3

D0574433

EXTREME ENTERTAINING
made simple

EXTREME

CONTRIBUTING WRITERS

Marley Majcher

Ronnda Hamilton

Sallie Crawford

Monica Cajayon

EVENT PLANNERS

Marley Majcher

Tom Bercu

Jennifer McGarigle

Oscar Maximillian Tucci

**EXECUTIVE CHEF—
RECIPE DEVELOPMENT**

Ronnda Hamilton

FOOD STYLIST

Alise Arato

**CD EXECUTIVE AND
CREATIVE PRODUCERS**

Eduardo Xol

Josh Young

Steve Miller

CD MUSICAL DIRECTOR

Josh Young

INVITATION AND MENU DESIGN

Keisha Beane

MAKEUP ARTIST

Carrie Merrick

ENTERTAINING
made simple

EDUARDO XOL

Cowritten by
STEVE MILLER

Photographed by
BILL AND KATHRYN WATSON

A CELEBRA BOOK

Celebra
Published by New American Library, a division of
Penguin Group (USA) Inc., 375 Hudson Street,
New York, New York 10014, USA
Penguin Group (Canada), 90 Eglinton Avenue East, Suite 700, Toronto,
Ontario M4P 2Y3, Canada (a division of Pearson Penguin Canada Inc.)
Penguin Books Ltd., 80 Strand, London WC2R 0RL, England
Penguin Ireland, 25 St. Stephen's Green, Dublin 2,
Ireland (a division of Penguin Books Ltd.)
Penguin Group (Australia), 250 Camberwell Road, Camberwell, Victoria 3124,
Australia (a division of Pearson Australia Group Pty. Ltd.)
Penguin Books India Pvt. Ltd., 11 Community Centre, Panchsheel Park,
New Delhi - 110 017, India
Penguin Group (NZ), 67 Apollo Drive, Rosedale, North Shore 0632,
New Zealand (a division of Pearson New Zealand Ltd.)
Penguin Books (South Africa) (Pty.) Ltd., 24 Sturdee Avenue,
Rosebank, Johannesburg 2196, South Africa

Penguin Books Ltd., Registered Offices:
80 Strand, London WC2R 0RL, England

First published by Celebra,
a division of Penguin Group (USA) Inc.

First Printing, November 2008
10 9 8 7 6 5 4 3 2 1

All photographs by Bill Watson and Kathryn Watson, except photographs on page 52 and top page 53 by Eduardo Xol.
Art on pages 13 and 14 by Eduardo Xol.

CELEBRA and logo are trademarks of Penguin Group (USA) Inc.

LIBRARY OF CONGRESS CATALOGING-IN-PUBLICATION DATA

Xol, Eduardo.
  Extreme entertaining made simple/Eduardo Xol; photography by Bill
and Kathryn Watson.
    p. cm.
  ISBN 978-0-451-22416-3
1. Parties. 2. Entertaining. I. Title.
GV1471.X65 2008
  793.2—dc22   2008010770

Set in Gotham Book
Designed by Pauline Neuwirth, Neuwirth & Associates, Inc.

PUBLISHER'S NOTE
The recipes contained in this book are to be followed exactly as written. The publisher is not responsible for your specific health or allergy needs that may require medical supervision. The publisher is not responsible for any adverse reactions to the recipes contained in this book.
    The publisher does not have any control over and does not assume any responsibility for author or third-party Web sites or their content.

I would like to dedicate this book to the memory of Catalina Marquez, who taught us all how to celebrate life! *Gracias*, Mama Catita! To the memory of Uncle Willy, Tia Chuy, and cousin Arcelia, you are always with us; to the Torres-Delgado family; and most of all, to the more than one hundred living members of the Catalina Marquez family residing in Los Angeles.

CONTENTS

EXTREME ENTERTAINING
made simple

*I*N MY FIRST book, *Home Sense*, I talk about a particular experience that served as the inspiration for my wanting to develop a philosophy about designing for the senses. During one of the episodes of *Extreme Makeover: Home Edition*, we were designing a home for a man who had gone blind. Our challenge was to design for all of the man's other senses so that he could get acclimated to his new situation as fast as possible. This is where and how I developed my philosophy for designing for the senses, and I have been designing this way ever since.

As I often say in the press, I've had many lives within this life of mine. I have reinvented myself several times, usually out of necessity. Oftentimes I have been questioned about my credentials as I have worked in my several careers and occupations. The path from that of "designer of homes" to that of "designer of events" has been a very easy one for me and one that has made perfect sense.

Several years ago, before my most recent resurrection on *Extreme Makeover: Home Edition* and shortly after the last incarnation of my music career, I was working several jobs to get myself back on my feet. I was teaching theater to kids, I was starting my landscape experience through gardening jobs and an internship, and I was also emceeing events on the weekends.

I worked for Disney Entertainment emceeing *quinceañeras*, weddings, and corporate events. In training for this job, I had to learn event planning. It was a great experience on many levels. I never would have guessed then that I would be using those skills to write this book, but then again, looking back at my life so far, I shouldn't be surprised at all. I have to admit, as I write this introduction from farmland in Wyoming, that I am laughing inside. Already in the process of putting this book together, I have had people question my credentials.

Truth be told, this was the book I wanted to write from the beginning, but my publisher thought it made more sense, no pun intended, to write a book about design first, since that is what I seemed to be most known for at the time. What makes me so excited about events and celebrations? Well, as with most things in my life, this "talent" was inherited through my family.

During the time that I was working at Disney Entertainment, my sister, Monica, became engaged to be married. She asked me if I would help her plan her wedding. I did. We designed every detail, including her dress. She wanted to be a princess for a day. I even composed and wrote original music to be played in the church during the ceremony. The piece "Fanfare to a Princess," which is on the CD accompanying this book, was from her wedding. The entire event was planned VERY specifically around my sister's personality, wants, and needs. Without knowing it, I had begun designing for the events and celebrating through the senses while planning her wedding. It would be many years before I would actually define this philosophy—a philosophy I now live by.

I strongly believe that every moment in life is an experience. And as such, an event that you design should be a truly singular experience. A great event will encompass all of the senses. But looking at the overall picture, it can be a bit overwhelming, so I learned early on to ask some basic questions:

1. What is the "look" and theme of the event? What type of environment will truly reflect this theme?

2. What should that environment smell like? What images do I want that smell to conjure up in the guests' minds? And how can that smell be re-created?

3. What types of food would represent this environment best? And what should it taste like?

4. What should the sound track to the event sound like? Are there music or types of sound that would best fit the event?

5. What would one expect to be touching in this environment? Can it be made fun? Luxurious? Intriguing?

And finally, after you've answered these questions or made your decisions:

6. Do your choices feel cohesive? Do they all make sense together?

Even with a few years of experience, I still sit down and think about each of these questions whether I'm attending an event as a guest or planning it. To incorporate this philosophy into your experiences, always ask yourself these types of questions. After a while, it will become second nature!

The concept of the special event has always been an important part of my family's DNA. I am now able to see that there has always been an influence of formality in the process of planning these events as well. Birthdays, holy days, and especially Mother's Day have always been big and important celebrations. For those of you who don't already know, I come from a family of four living generations in Los Angeles. There are just over 120 living members in my family, and believe it or not, we ALL get together on a fairly regular basis. The most important holiday in my family, which has become our "family reunion," is Mother's Day. Why? Partially because the Mexican culture is very matriarchal. My family is also very matriarchal, being that my maternal grandmother had seven daughters and most of my first cousins are also women.

As our family grew, so did the Mother's Day event. Quickly, my parents' home became the permanent location for the party. What had started as a potluck with the stereo playing a wide variety of music eventually turned into a very well thought-out and orchestrated day that was custom catered with live music, a carefully chosen menu, and beautifully coordinated decor!

My father, who is extremely organized, is most responsible for turning the event into the formal gathering it is now. When I use the word "formal," I'm not talking about tuxedos and china, but rather an event that was well planned with invitations, a budget, an RSVP list, and conceptual designs. My father made checklists, categorized activities, created budgets, and started planning up to ten months in advance to be sure that every detail was attended to. Once my father had retired and mostly in the last couple of years, my siblings and I started becoming more and more involved. We've now split up the tasks as a family and have our system down pat! However, I still try to fine-tune the event, year after year. After all, the family is only going to grow. In fact, many of the in-laws now bring their families as well. In time, I see the event moving to a larger, more appropriate space. It's getting crowded at my parents' house!

This brings me to the fact that I love to entertain people. I now realize that the best entertaining must encompass all of the senses in a way that is cohesive. Good food and drink, great visual and tactile decor, the right smell, and a wonderful sound track can make or break any event, no matter how big or small. But proper planning is key. So many times people just throw something together. Not to say that an impromptu gathering should be avoided, as oftentimes these can be the best parties ever, but most of the time, if you know you're throwing a party, a checklist and careful planning can ensure the party's success.

Decorum and etiquette can also make or break a party. An event should always have an actual start time when everything is in place. When the first guest arrives, everything should be just right! I can't tell you how many times I've been to a party where the host was running late—not good!

In this book I hope to show you examples of templates that can work for many types of events. I will discuss how to go about planning a party while designing it at the same time. I will review the cohesive concept of entertaining for all of the senses and the etiquette that is necessary to be sure that any event is a great success. I've teamed up with several well-known event planners, each with his own individual perspective. Together we've created unique and exciting ideas that will hopefully inspire you to create your own. After all, this is just a guide and an example. I've said before that we are all our own lives' designers—we are also the planners of our own special events. They are the ongoing events of our lives. Events are about celebrations, and I invite you to celebrate life, celebrate yourselves, and celebrate your family and friends, all through the senses!

celebrating through the senses

SOME PEOPLE WOULD say that our greatest assets are the five senses: sight, hearing, touch, smell, and taste. When we apply these senses, we find that we open ourselves to powerful, intuitive insights that help us make sense of the world around us. Our instincts have taken us quite far, and because of them, we humans have learned how to live efficiently with the elements of the environment.

The same concept can be applied when it comes to creating the look and ambience of an event or party. In fact, your first instinct should be to draw inspiration from the five senses. Doing so is your first step in creating unforgettable moments, which is what we all want to achieve for any celebration in life. It has been stated that the best events are the ones that your guests will remember for years. The senses play a significant role when it comes to memory. Simply smelling a scent can bring the vivid details of a moment, or hearing a song can transport someone to a time long forgotten.

In this book, I will show you how to use your five senses as your main inspiration when designing any event and how these techniques can be used over and over again and toward all types of occasions. The six parties—Classic Dinner Party, Princess Party, Spa Party, White Party, Margarita Party, and Summer Party—were all designed by me and my team, and they have been previously executed for clients, friends, and family. These events were chosen because of their all-encompassing themes and versatility. As you will see from the detailed account of each of the parties, from the conception of the event to table setting, you'll find the planning to be cost effective and easy for anyone to execute. Also, for each event, I will show you how I applied each sense to enrich and elevate the look and themes. You'll see that these senses will take you far in planning your event. From a simple dinner party to a grand event, such as a wedding, you'll have the resources and techniques to execute any plan and know how to apply your senses and personal touch!

And as a general rule for all designers and creators, it is always a good idea to take a moment after every event to recap and think about how all the design elements came together and how each sense contributed to the overall ambience and feel of the party. This is a technique and tip that's as important as learning to apply all the senses. What with the preparation and hosting time, it's likely you won't have a moment to appreciate these details. Not only does this allow you to take part in the success of your party, but it also allows you to gain a sense of your own design style and method.

VISION

*M*Y HOUSE IS definitely a reflection of who I am. I can't wait to get home, grab a good book, put on some music, light a candle, and collapse on my couch. Traveling, which I do A LOT of, wears me down, and there is nothing better than being in a place where I can relax. On the ottomans in front of my couch and on my tables, I keep a stack of magazines and books as well as fresh orchids. The orchids bring the outside in and remind me of my mother, who cultivated them for many years. I've always been surrounded by gardens and nature. The earth tones and neutral colors that I have introduced to my home environment keep me grounded and calm. Work follows me everywhere, even in my home, but when needed, I turn off the computer and my PDA and take a step back from the day's work. My environment helps me do that.

I know that my house is comfortable for me to live in, but I also want it to be suitable for others to enjoy themselves in as well. I make sure to leave space for guests to walk around and talk to one another so they don't feel the need to stay in one place. My family and I try to get together as much as possible, but we all have busy schedules, so it is a blessing when we can all meet for dinner. Whether I am entertaining family or friends, I encourage my guests to feel at home, so I set up different spaces where they can sit while talking among themselves. Regardless of how your house is set up, there is always a way in which you can make the space seem roomier than it is. Putting unnecessary objects away in a storage area so that you will have more space to put out drinks or food is a start. Rearranging furniture so there is more space to walk around is another, but just uncluttering your space will be a major improvement.

One of the most important senses in design and entertaining is the sense of sight. That which we see usually gives us our first impression, not excluding intuition of course. Colors, visual textures, and composition can really pull an event together visually. Below are some theories on color. Many of them were part of my first book, but I have elaborated on their direct correlation to how they would function for an event.

> One of the most important senses in design and entertaining is the sense of sight. That which we see usually gives us our first impression.

Neutral Colors allow other, more vibrant colors to come to the forefront and shine while also helping to tone down a palette that might be too strong on its own. Neutral colors include variations of black, white, brown, beige, and gray. The nice thing about these colors is that they work in many different environments and won't necessarily overpower your color scheme, no matter what the event is. Although neutral on their own, black and white together are almost universally related to formality.

Cool Colors though sometimes cold and sterile can also be fun and even comforting. These colors include neutrals, like whites and grays, but also include blues and greens, which would tend to be higher on the comfort scale. These are natural feeling colors that would be good for a relaxed environment.

Warm Colors tend to make you feel comfortable and secure in your environment. For many people sunlight and meadows of wildflowers come to mind when they are asked what they think warm colors represent. In fact warm colors are more in the yellow, orange, and red categories, which can bring up many emotions ranging from love to anger. When I think of warm colors, I think of romance and autumn.

Earth Tones draw from the subtle and neutral color scheme found in the natural colors of the Earth. Think grass, fresh tilled soil, forests, and deserts, which bring to mind brown, tan, gray, green, and variations of those colors. Many times soft reds will be included.

Pastel Colors are the mediators of the color wheel. They're friendly and they don't get into many arguments with other colors. They bridge lighter and darker colors, not to mention varied textures, and they tend to bring balance and a sense of calm to a room. Like neutral colors, they bring out more prominent colors and have no problem taking a backseat to a more vibrant palette. The interesting thing about pastels is that these colors bring a bit of formality to a room but at the same time don't make the space feel stodgy and old. As a matter of fact you can create an eclectic and vibrant statement with pastels as fast as you can create an enveloping and soft surrounding. I like pastels for events that may want to bring back periods of the past, and they are perfect for children's parties and parties for females.

Monochromatic Colors are the different shadings of a single color. I love rooms and accessories that are all the same colors, since they make such a dramatic statement. Some people feel designing in monochromatic colors is boring and lacks imagination, but I feel just the opposite. I think it is elegant and clean. Done the right way, a space can look magical and truly chic and sophisticated. You need to be a bit daring. Using hues of the same color is also a great way to set the mood for an event or a living space. If you are looking to highlight various architectural aspects of a space, then painting in a single color or subtle variations thereof would not be the best of choices, since a single color won't make anything in particular stand out, but will make the whole room cohesive. Going monochromatic can work for just about any event!

Colors can make you feel energized, calm, worried, hungry, or happy. Surrounding yourself with a mix of colors will create a place in which you can feel  comfortable. Personally, greens seem to be easier on my eyes. I like the rich green of aloe plants and dark forest greens, as well. Being the color of grass and leaves, green connects me to the outside. And the fact that green is said to be the color of growth and prosperity is not a bad thing. I'm a very social person, but when I'm home relaxing, I like being able to let my thoughts run free as I spend my free time in solitude, and these colors help me do so.

Have you ever wondered why you feel relaxed when you're in contact with blue? Navy and dark blues are symbols of power and authority. They are solid and concrete. We see policemen and officers of all sorts wearing navy blue shades, showing the grounded nature of their jobs. Light blues differ a bit in their significance. These colors are a reflection of the sky and represent the passing of the dark night. In ancient days, our ancestors looked to the sky to tell time and to see that they had made it through the dark and obtrusive night.

Purple is well known as the color of royalty. Centuries ago, not just anyone  could lay their paws on a piece of purple clothing. When the dye was first used, it was very hard to come by and therefore extremely expensive. The color has not lost its touch and is seen as a color signifying power and wealth. War heroes and survivors are awarded Purple Hearts, in recognition of their valiant and brave efforts. Purple is a great color to add to a neutral palette.

As for the other side of the color spectrum, everyone knows that red is a symbol of love and extreme feelings. This color is important because of its intense effect on people's emotions. It is also the color of blood. When we see a stop sign or red light, we have an immediate reaction, but why was the stop sign designed the way it was? Red is bright and obtrusive, causing in our bodies a psychological reaction to pay attention. Needless to say, the color red is used sparingly as a primary design color but frequently as an accent color. So, if you are throwing a party other than one associated with love or relationships, it is probably not the best idea to use an abundant amount of red. As a Latino, I grew up with a lot of red around, but it was always joined by other colors, such as yellow, orange, and green. They are vibrant colors that reflect my heritage and the personalities of my family. Latinos are very passionate, displaying red proudly in order to show strength and energy. Many other cultures use red as well to display these same characteristics. It is a bold color that displays vigor and determination.

We all want our guests to mingle and feel comfortable while getting to know one another. Yellow is a color that will do just that. It encourages communication. It commands our attention with its vibrancy, like red or orange, but it also makes us feel more confident and optimistic. Popping out from the surrounding colors, it will spark creative thoughts and energy. Whenever I step outside and see that the sun is shining, the day starts on a good note.

I also love colors that reflect the gardens that I used to work in with my family. Bright greens complemented by bold browns flood my rooms, creating my own private haven. Designing with plants and flowers is one of the best ways to fill your home with natural color. A great arrangement on the kitchen table or a tall lush green plant in the corner of a room will add a sense of calm to your environment. Designing with color is one of the most exciting things for me to do. There are so many tangibles to play with when designing with color, each triggering emotions and altering moods. Thus it is obvious when I write that color selection is a powerful part in planning any celebration.

There are so many ways that you can accent your room with touches of color that can be both subtle and sly. Set the appetizers on a yellow platter and give mixed drinks a punch by adding exotic fruit slices that have some great vibrant colors. At any party you throw, each component, from the plates to napkins, floral displays to parting gifts, should relate to the others, whether color or theme . . . but don't be afraid to step out of your comfort zone. When having a few good friends over, to make things more laid back, try mixing and matching different colors. For example, your plates can be a variety of colors and textures by taking your grandma's vintage china and combining it with two-dollar flea market finds. Glasses can also be a mixed bag of colored glass, while your tablecloth can be something unique and thematic. Friends will love the arrangements. Stories behind the decorations are bound to come out, but again, keep to your theme and color combinations defined to tie everything together.

When it comes to seasonal parties, it's great when it feels like winter during Christmas. The snow outside and the crackling of the freshly cut logs in the fireplace are great incentives that will surely set the mood, but should you be living in Tuscany, Las Vegas, or Maui, for that matter, there doesn't have to be snow on the ground in order to bring winter in. Use a great assortment of silver vases and accessories, and add a light blue tablecloth, and you have yourself the start of a winter wonderland. These colors will make your guests shiver with delight! Collect as many shimmering and glittering objects that you can find to place around the room. For a centerpiece, you could use a large glass bowl filled with clear marbles, feathers, or even ice! To add to the magic, sprinkle the tablecloth and centerpiece with glitter or throw some sparkling faux gemstones around the place settings. Take some glittery silver or light blue fabric and drape it over the sofa or armchairs. You will get the effect of rolling hills covered in snow. I will further explore the sense of sound later, but many objects can be useful to cover more than one sense. Wrapping a light blue ribbon around the napkins and attaching a little silver bell to it will add a jingle to the party and remind us of the season. Include some fake snow to the mix, and you have a chilling scene!

SOUND

There are two ways to create a sound track for an event: around the party's theme or based on the appeal of your guests.

I TEND TO believe that there are very few designers who consider sound when working on a project. Event planners are a different story. Music is usually an integral part of any event or celebration. In bigger events, many times an event planner will find someone to handle the music separately, as in a DJ, which can often challenge the cohesion of an event. In small home gatherings, many times music planning is left to the end—an afterthought fulfilled by whatever can be found on the radio or in the CD cases.

Sound is extremely important to me for a couple of reasons. First of all, music is my first language. Second, I have been able to identify my strongest intelligence as being musical. I learn and experience the world through my hearing first . . . after my intuition, that is. ☺

As I write this section of my book, I find myself in Maine working on *Extreme Makeover: Home Edition.* I am looking out the window of my trailer and have a view of the nearby mountains and beautiful green trees. My sound track currently consists of the wind blowing through the trees mixed with wood shop equipment and the beeping of construction vehicles. For my personal experience, the sound track is fitting. If I were a neighbor, however, it might not be as comforting. It all depends on one's expectation.

I can't tell you how many times I've gone to a great restaurant with great food and a wonderful design, but the sound track is all wrong. Then there are the times where everything is perfect, including the music. I have a great friend by the name of Jesse Acevedo, who is an artist, designer, and filmmaker. He was a former restaurateur and producer, and we worked together in restaurants in San Francisco and in entertainment in Latin America. He had a restaurant in San Francisco called Pozole, and he was very "hands on" about its development and success. He designed the interiors, created the menu, and programmed the music. The vibe was Latin, sexy, fun, and delicious. The place was packed and had lines of people waiting to get in. Why? Well for one, the food was great, but also because the event of going there was a cohesive one. You walked into an environment, not just a restaurant, and you were transported into Jesse's world! Indigo blue walls framed a room filled with candlelight and statues of papier-mâché figures towered over the diners as they were served by beautiful exotic people from all over the world. Delicious food with influences from Mexico and Latin America was accompanied by a blend of Latin-flavored dance music and sangria that was constantly being poured so you never had an empty glass until it was time for you to leave. This, my friends, was one of the best experiences of my life and one that would influence my event planning forever. Jesse, again I say, *gracias*!

In Los Angeles, the first thing I do when I get to my office or my home is light a candle and turn on some music. When I throw a party, no matter how big or small, I will create a playlist specific to the event. For example, if I am hosting my family, it will be a combination of salsa, standard Latin ballads or boleros, and pop, funk, and disco from the seventies and eighties. If the party is for my "Euro" friends, I'll choose a nice mix of samba and electronic dance music. If I were to throw a party for my mates on the set of *Extreme Makeover: Home Edition* . . . wow, is it ever interesting! It would be a very eclectic mix of country, rock, and hip-hop.

There are two ways to create a sound track for an event: around the party's theme or based on the appeal of your guests. If you're throwing a party and serving Latin food, play Spanish-language music! There is also instrumental world music that would be perfect for any type of international-themed party. But first, before making a decision, ask yourself what the demographics of your guests are. Are they twenty-, thirty-, or fifty somethings? Do they like to dance? Have they traveled? Once you answer these questions, it will be easy to put together a playlist that your guests will enjoy and that will make your party a success.

Remember to take the time to plan your sound track. Sit down, take inventory of your theme and guests, listen to music, and make a list. Try it out in advance to see how it really sounds. You might be surprised at your reaction to music in a collection. After all, we oftentimes are drawn to a song that stands alone, but it may not fit into a collection or for a particular event. For example, an upbeat and fast dance song is perfect for a number of events while a song about heartbreak will rarely be appropriate for a party.

You may want to enlist or hire a person to assist with your musical programming. Just be sure that they are following your directions. After all, it is your party! Another thing to consider is sound quality. This is another area that is oftentimes handled by a professional to alleviate stress, although nowadays an iPod and some speakers can create the sound track for any event almost anywhere.

As I mentioned before, music is my first language. My mother says I was humming, singing, and imitating people's tones of voice before I ever uttered a word. Music has been an important part of my life, which is why I wanted to produce the accompanying CD sampler. Here I have collected two songs for each of the events that are in this book. These are examples that I feel would be appropriate for the festivities. You can add to these and create your own collection from what music you have or would like to purchase. I hope you enjoy the collection!

While contemplating all of the information in this section, ask yourself a question: What is your personal sound track?

perfect seasonal centerpiece. Pumpkins smell great and are large enough for candles, flowers, or aromatic oils to be placed inside of. With a little thought and creativity, many different fall arrangements can be made using pumpkins, gourds, leaves, and other edible foods. Branches from trees that bloom best in autumn are another innovative and fun way to dress a table. Pussy willows or oak branches with great yellow and red leaves can be interlaced with other flowers to create a fall theme that is fresh and new and will surely impress your guests. This truly brings the outside in, and will allow for a nice woodsy scent. Have fun with these arrangements. Nothing you create will be wrong, so you might as well do something outside of your comfort zone. The colors of fall, such as browns, reds, yellows, and oranges, will make for a warm and intoxicating environment.

It truly depends on the mood that you would like to set for your event. If it's a more romantic setting you are going for, turn down the lights and set out dozens of candles around the rooms you will be entertaining in. Make half of them scented and half unscented. Immediately, the smells should envelop, not overwhelm. If you are throwing a sit-down affair, I would suggest that after the main course has been cleared away, you allow your guests to cleanse their palates. The smell and taste of mint will clear the senses and allow your guests to get ready for the next part of the celebration: dessert! If asking your guests to chew on mint is not an appealing option, then think about handing out a small hand towel that has been lightly dipped in mint and water. The fresh scent will definitely be appreciated.

What smells trigger your happiest memories? A fun exercise is to write down a few things that smell good and make you smile. Go out and try to bring these items into your home and office. It's amazing what the simplest of things can do. Use this as a design exercise as well. Try to incorporate your ideas into a new fresh palette for your rooms. Here's hoping that a fresh scent will assist in capturing the lifestyle you've always wanted both at home on a day-to-day basis, as well as during your entertaining experiences.

TASTE

There is a particular essence that one tastes, smells, and feels from the food prepared by those who love us. To define this essence is to know the person.

*C*LOSE YOUR EYES and picture yourself eating your favorite foods. Maybe you're on the couch with a good book and a gallon of double chocolate malted crunch ice cream, or in the car eating some takeout French fries with just the right amount of salt and ketchup on them. For those of you who are a bit healthier, picking at slices of papaya with some lime, lightly salted and sprinkled with chili flakes, might be just right. In my case it would be double-layered *pastel de tres leches* with a heaping sprinkling of cinnamon. I don't do it often, but since we are talking about our favorites, I had to be honest.

Is your mouth watering yet? Regardless of your food of choice, even before it enters your mouth, your taste buds get all tingly with anticipation. It's weird but they know something good is coming. Food for me is a conversation starter. New friends are made while cooking in the kitchen or lingering over a great meal. I love to throw dinner parties, and I especially love experimenting with new recipes. Since I am on the road so much, dinner parties are a great way for me to reconnect with intimate groups of friends and family at one time. And because I am always curious to see how people live in their personal spaces, watching interactions between people, especially around a small table, makes for great theater. I've found that when the atmosphere is right people feel more relaxed, and therefore they open up a bit more about themselves and their lives. I try to have a small group of people I am close to come over before the rest of the guests arrive, and we chill out in the kitchen while I prepare the food. I find that even people who don't cook—I'm talking about those who never set foot in the kitchen and can only make a good reservation—love helping out and being involved in the night's festivities. There is a reason that in the United States the room where most people congregate during a party is the kitchen. If the food is good, it's because they want to be first when the appetizers come out of the oven. But I also think that kitchens bring back great memories for people. Family and food usually bring smiles to people's faces.

When I was younger I spent a lot of time in my father's and grandmother's gardens and my mother's and grandmother's kitchens. I felt safe in these places, and this is where I connected with my elders. The kitchen for me was the sacred place where we cooked, ate, and shared. We always sat down to eat together and nobody left until all were done. Currently, I don't have a kitchen large enough for one of those eight-foot-long country pine wood tables that I love, but someday I will. I have to!

As for what food to serve and what drinks to pair the edibles with, think about the theme of the party. You certainly wouldn't serve salmon steaks at a child's birthday. We chose to highlight some delicious food by creating innovative menus that will complement and elevate an event. Along with the visual display of the table settings and floral displays, the food most definitely sets the tone, first in taste, then also in sight and smell.

Proper lighting, beautiful flowers, and scented candles are always important elements for having a wonderful party, but it goes without saying that if the food is bad or the wine has seen better days, no matter what you do, the party will ultimately be remembered for inedible cuisine. All that hard work in preparing the night in Tuscany or your niece's graduation party will be ruined along with the steak filets that you seasoned with that "something special" you found while on vacation. Ten years from now, you and the event will still be brought up in conversation, but it won't be about your decorating prowess or your party-planning innovations. Unfortunately, it will be about the bad food.

There is a particular essence that one tastes, smells and feels from the food prepared by those who love us. To define this essence is to know the person. And to have known my grandmother, Mama Catita, and to have shared in the many special *antojitos* she prepared was to have understood her grace, humility, resourcefulness, and sense of humor, and the sheer delight she took in enjoying the smells of the kitchen.

In the 1940s, Catalina Marquez was left alone in Mexico, raising seven daughters by herself. Prayers sustained her spirits and those of her daughters when there was no food to be divided. But not every day was a desperate one. When Catalina made enough money from cleaning houses and sewing dresses for her wealthy neighbors, she took pleasure in creating meals of beef, garlic, onions, and red chili for her daughters and anyone else who cared to join them. The reality was that her delicious warm stews consisted of more tomatoes and onions than beef, since meat was so expensive, nevertheless Catalina knew how to make a little of a great ingredient go a long way. It was the same with her desserts. Some sugar and cinnamon sprinkled over a fried tortilla was enough to make delicious *buñuelos*.

Poverty made Catalina resourceful and wonderfully creative. Long before immigrating to the United States, Catalina took to growing her own herbs and fruit trees. She was as meticulous about her garden as she was about her home. "You must take great care of what you do have," she always said. Her gardens bore figs, limes, lemons, oranges, little kumquats, mint, oregano, and basil. She used her fruits to make *agua fresca*, or sweetened water drinks, and her herbs for teas, soups, and salsas. Whatever the treat, my grandmother was always willing to share it. It was the same for her funny stories and sayings, or *dichos*.

Life became much easier for Catita once she came to the United States because her daughters were adamant about supporting her. They didn't want to see her struggle anymore. So for the first time she indulged in buying blocks of cocoa, bunches of cinnamon sticks, coffee-filled candies, a variety of chilis, steaks, and goat meat, too. It was from this point onward that her cooking really flourished. She remembered some of the dishes she had eaten as a child and re-created them in her own way. These re-creations gave birth to a family tradition of getting together during holidays and helping my grandmother prepare special foods like tamales, chiles rellenos, moles, sopes, and various desserts. We always took her lead and sat around long rectangular tables, each of us with a particular task; some of us cleaned cornhusks, some ground chili paste into a traditional *molcajete*, and others prepared tamales for steaming. Year after year, Mama Catita, which is what all her grandchildren called her, shared her recipes with her daughters and grandchildren. It was during these special cooking gatherings in the kitchen that we all caught up with family gossip, and learned a little more about one another and our grandmother.

The tradition of preparing good food, loving one another, and welcoming friends and neighbors to our family feasts survived my grandmother. Over the years, the recipes, like time and the younger generations of our family, have evolved to include new twists on old favorites. There is no doubt that Mama Catita has been the guiding force behind my making sure that the sense of taste is always and forever taken into serious consideration whenever planning any event, no matter how big or how small!

THE SIXTH SENSE: INTUITION

Our intuition is a window into our personalities and character.

*T*HIS SECTION WOULD not be complete without including the elusive sixth sense, or what I like to think of as intuition or "gut feeling." When we arrive at an event, our sense of intuition allows us to connect a chain of thoughts that occur together in an instant. These thoughts occur at an initial glance or entrance to a party. It immediately gives us a general feeling as the rest of our senses communicate to one another. What I'm saying is a bit abstract, I know, but it is extremely relevant. Everyone has heard the saying that first impressions are the most important. However true this may be, those first thoughts about a person, place, thing, or event are crucial to the forming of our feelings, beliefs, and judgments.

Unfortunately, many people ignore this sixth sense. Truth be told, many people are afraid of it. Sometimes the process happens so quickly that we don't even know that it is happening at all. It is a flash of comfort or discomfort that sparks inside of us like magic. It makes us confront the truth. Forming our intuition and coming to trust it is much more simple than it seems. I first started concretely using my sixth sense as a child, but as I grew older, my connection to it became more distant. It wasn't until a few years ago that I again began to become very confident in what I sensed and what I believed in. That's when I realized that I had not fully put all of my trust into my intuition for most of my adult life.

During a period of change a few years ago, which included a career and relationship transition, I was exposed to a lot of other people's criticism; my family, friends, and professional critics all gave me their opinions and shared their beliefs with me as I entered new and uncharted territories. The criticism I experienced was ultimately very beneficial to my personal and professional growth, but I have to admit that it was often very painful. We all need to hear feedback about our ideas and about the decisions that we make, but I had never been confronted with such an abundant amount of judgment about my life and work choices before then. While some people congratulated me for my resilience, most continued to criticize me with harsh voices and sometimes even with silence.

During this time I realized that creating a new life for oneself is much like the experience of trying a new recipe. When you're attempting to cook something new, you want it to be the absolute best, using the ingredients that make it delicious but original at the same time. But you're probably not the only one who is going to enjoy this recipe, as I'm sure you want whoever else is eating it to be blown away, right? After all, when you're trying a new recipe, it usually means that it is for you and others . . . not for you alone. Often it takes a little time and effort to find the perfect balance. You have your mom handing you her recipes, while your friends and colleagues are throwing their favorite ingredients at you at the same time. Trying a bunch of them is the key. Take what you have been given, but more important, create a dish that is specific to what will represent you best while still tasting great to your friends. Trusting your intuition to let you know when you've balanced your ingredients properly is the key. As with anything, this is easy for some people and takes a few tries for other people.

Our intuition is a window into our personalities and character. Think about it. Our first thoughts are a quick judgment of what we see, hear, smell, touch, and taste, and for most of us, it is all of these things at the same time. Staying true to that "first feeling" that you get when you interact with someone or something is a valuable tool to have. We should also take into consideration that our intuition is not only the feeling that we get from our first reactions, but many times it can encompass the feelings that we hold on to for long periods of time. There is no need to "jump the gun" at your first thoughts, because many times the initial feelings will stay with you longer than just a few minutes. How will you know when to wait a while? Trust me. Trust yourself. You will know.

Here is the irony, though: We usually use our intuition most when we know we don't like or trust something. It becomes a valuable defense mechanism. Sadly, for many people that is where it stays.

Many people these days are discouraging the use of their positive intuition, dismissing it as part of the New Age movement of the past, but I am completely confident in it and urge others to trust theirs, as well. Embrace this gift, and don't let anyone steer you away from it. It is the best way to stay true to yourself, not only when designing or throwing an event, but also in your everyday life. By putting faith in this sense, you will be able to bring your character into everything that comes your way.

Our first design and planning ideas are usually the freshest, and our intuition is one of the greatest tools we can use in that process. You're walking around a shopping mall looking for something to wear to the dinner party that you are hosting, and you pass by a store that looks like it has some interesting knickknacks. You can't help but check out what they have inside. It will just take a second. It's amazing how many compliments I have received on the little pieces that I have found in unexpected places. From weekend garage sales to upscale department stores, I can always find something to spice up the design of an event. Using your intuition to mix and match pieces allows you to be daring with your setups, creating an environment and space that is comforting yet intriguing at the same time. Does the ribbon wrapped around the vase ruin the rustic look that you were trying to pull off? Take it off! Chances are, your reaction to an addition or subtraction to your layout speaks the truth. Be confident with your feelings according to your reactions, and the party will be a success, for your guests will feel the same thing you do. Their intuition will be in line with yours. Your event will be well balanced, and your guests will be thrilled. It will be a success!

I was just in Wyoming working on an episode of *Extreme Makeover: Home Edition*. We had installed an entertainment center against a wall that was twenty-two feet high. We were behind schedule, and the cameras were to roll in at any time. The problem was that from the second floor, you could see exposed wires and unpainted surfaces on top of the entertainment center. There was no time to paint or to call in any more contractors or painters before the family came home. It would have to be permanently fixed later, but, in the meantime, my first thought was to go outside and cut a bunch of pine trees and cover the top of the entertainment center with them. Then the negative voices in my head said, "That's foolish!" Not five minutes later, a design producer asked me if I would approve of a production assistant going outside and cutting a bunch of branches to cover the top of the entertainment center. They did it, and it looked fantastic. You see, I was right, but I didn't trust my sixth sense!

Our intuition is our simplest and most complex sense all at once. I do believe that it is a choice to recognize it and use it or not. In order for our intuition to be fully functioning, all of the other senses need to be considered and fine-tuned. Our reaction to a certain setting comes from the combination of emotions evoked due to our five senses. What does the room smell like? What makes it smell like this? Are you conscious of how you feel about it and why? Are our senses even engaged? Does the smell make sense with what you see? What music is playing? Is it the proper sound track for the environment? In a flash, all of these things should always be considered. Questioning why you feel the way you do takes your intuition to the next level, and these inquiries are dependent on the alertness of our senses. That is not to say that people who are not able to see or hear—the senses we take so much for granted—are less able to use their other senses to connect to their intuition. It is quite the opposite, actually. In order for their intuition to be in tune, they have to pay attention to all of the senses they do have more carefully, and they usually do.

The greatest way that I have allowed my sixth sense to guide me has been in my identifying myself as being synesthetic. When I began designing, I used my experience in musical composition to help guide me in visual composition. This is the reason I am actually in a place with my life and my career that allows me to write this second book. My sixth sense allowed me to believe that my visual and auditory wires were "crossed." I could hear what I saw, and I could see what I heard. This rare condition has also allowed me to trust my gut more than most. I trust my feelings and do my best to use them in all aspects of my life, i.e., design, entertaining, relationships, and lifestyle.

Tap into your intuition. We all have it; whether we listen to our intuition is the real question. Breathe in deeply and clear your mind. Have fun with using your intuition when designing. Let your personality flow and come out in your creations. At the end of the day, it all comes down to one thing: Do you trust yourself to create the recipe you really want to challenge yourself to make? Do you dare to design the party that you truly want to have? Of course you do! Take that great spirit of yours holding all of those bright ideas and mix and match them together. You will be amazed at how much you can accomplish by simply letting your intuition take over and by allowing your free-flowing creative thoughts to release themselves. It will make your house a more comfortable place for you to live and entertain in; your personality and ideas will be reflected in everything that you design. So let your mind run wild, and when you see that set of eclectic colorful serving plates, or when you want to use a different glass at every place setting, follow your intuition!

classic dinner party

APPROPRIATE FOR:

Business Networking

Getting Together with Friends

Singles' Mixers

THROWING A SIMPLE dinner party can cause nights of sleeplessness. Believe me, I know. I've been awake at three a.m., trying to go through all the stupid scenarios one can think of. What if the food is lousy? What if the guests don't get along? Is the music setting the right tone? Do I use scented candles? Will the chandelier be okay? Do I invest in some very good wine, or is a simple chardonnay sufficient? There comes a point when you just have to let everything be. Planning, however, is the key ingredient to any great dinner party. That and a few good stories to keep the guests interested.

Think about a theme for the evening, the food you want to serve, the colors of the flowers in the centerpiece, and the music that will set the tone. If you make it all complement one another, things will be seamless, and the party will be a huge success, with your guests talking about your prowess in the kitchen as well as your eye for design. For the most part, I have no doubt that you know what works well together. You know what you like and dislike. Don't prepare foods that you wouldn't be happy about being served or, for that matter, cleaning up. You don't have to be a Cordon Bleu chef to make some really killer appetizers and entrées that will taste as good as they smell. In a crunch, specialty food stores have truly beautiful dishes that are easy to prepare and can be arranged in a visually stunning way on the plate. So don't freak out.

Much like family get-togethers, a dinner party is a way for me to catch up with my friends in between my travels. I try to keep the list to under ten people so I can comfortably talk to everyone and make sure everyone has my complete attention. With that said, I feel that the Classic Dinner Party is perfect for a small group of four, or even for a group as large as twelve. If there are more than a dozen people at a table, it may become difficult to manage a sit-down dinner on your own, plus most people would have to set up an additional table, which means certain guests would be separated from the group, which is no fun. We're not talking about kids' tables here.

Also, when I make my guest list, I try to invite people not everyone is familiar with. It makes for better conversation when people are interested in learning about one another. There is nothing wrong with being a conduit for new friendships and even business opportunities. The most successful dinner parties I have are those that get everyone involved in the process. I don't mean that I put the guests to work, however I never have everything done prior to people arriving. I love when my friends, coworkers, and family gather in my kitchen. Kitchens hold that unique space in people's homes. No matter how big or small the kitchen, everyone ends up in there. I think most people want to get the lowdown on what is coming out of the oven for the main course so they can decide whether to fill up on appetizers! But getting back to my point about having guests over while I am still preparing: I've found that people enjoy helping out a little since it makes them feel vested in the party. It is also a great way for people to mingle before sitting down at the table.

During the actual dinner, I go around the table and introduce everyone and ask them about anything exciting happening in their lives. It makes them feel good that I'm interested and gives them a chance to glow a little bit in front of the other guests. People get genuinely excited for one another, and it can be somewhat inspirational for others to think about. I understand that we hope to impress people when throwing a dinner. It is nerve-racking, but fear is a good thing sometimes. You'll pay attention to detail and, I have no doubt, make it the best gathering you have ever had.

I was lucky enough to be raised in a family in which we always sat down together at a table to eat when my father got home from work. Before my mother went back to school and started our family business, and while she was still very much domestic, she would prepare a meal every day. I remember music playing in the background as she cooked. I was usually the one who set the table with linens, silverware, and glassware. Nothing fancy, mind you, but the ritual took place every day. My father would get home after a long commute and a long day of hard work, and after greeting my brother, sister, and me, he would retreat upstairs to "decompress." My mother insisted we give him some time alone and would keep us busy finishing the preparation for dinner so that our feelings wouldn't get hurt. Like magic, it seemed that dinner was ready when my father was. We would sit down together and eat and converse about our day, and we would get up from the table when everyone was finished.

My family's dinner rituals taught me valuable insights on social dynamics, and I continue to learn by observing the ways in which others construct their events or dinner. The Classic Dinner Party was inspired by a party that my friend Count Oscar Maximillian Tucci hosted at his villa in Florence. Max comes from a long line of restaurateurs, philanthropists, and social entertainers. His grandfather founded the famous restaurant Delmonico's in New York City. His talent for creating detailed and beautiful table arrangements was the main reason why I asked him to help with this dinner party. The same theme is reflected in the intricate coral center table piece—an image Max conjured up while thinking about his experience flying over the most beautiful coral reef in the Pacific Ocean.

We wanted to keep it small and intimate, and we would invite people who, for the most part, didn't know one another. They would get acquainted during this experience, and Max and I wanted to make it unique, memorable, and educational. I truly wanted my guests to be able to take away ideas that they would then be able to do themselves.

VISION | coral reefs

ONE OF THE reasons that Max suggested that we have our Classic Dinner Party at our friend actress Eva La Rue's home was based on his inspiration. As I mentioned before, Max had taken inspiration for the design of this event from flying over beautiful coral reefs on a recent trip. When he pointed out to me that Eva's dining room had murals with a seashell theme, we decided that it would be the perfect backdrop for our dinner.

In general, the colors of the room were a cross between a tan-brown, beige, and a hint of peach. The light fixture was a dome of glass in beige and brown with whimsical patterns and circles; it had a starfishlike point at the center. The chairs Eva had bought were of beige upholstery and medium-brown wood. They had arched backs and were extremely comfortable. They were of a fairly large size, so a party of six would be the maximum allowed around the table. All in all, the room was the perfect size for our intimate get-together.

We chose to shop at Waterford-Wedgwood online for our tabletop, and chose this amazing crystal, Fidelity by Vera Wang for Wedgwood, so I carefully took each glass and inspected it for labels before getting it ready to be washed.

the centerpiece

The concept for the entire Classic Dinner Party was based around the centerpiece of the table. In most instances, you wouldn't necessarily want to create an obstruction to conversation across the table, but in this case it was purposeful. We were going to invite six people who didn't really know one another. Only a few did. We were going to intentionally seat strangers we thought would be compatible next to one another. This seating arrangement with the giant centerpiece would encourage people sitting next to one another to converse the most. This is a great way to initiate people into getting to know one another. The easiest part about our plan is that we knew where the conversation would start: the centerpiece, naturally!

Max and I discussed the centerpiece at length, and he created a base for us to work from together. The primary elements were the nautical ones. Looking at the centerpiece, I was reminded of being on a boat somewhere back in time. The nautical elements mixed with the elements of the Old World and modern glamour made it very romantic. From a craft store, we picked up a sea net for under ten dollars and used it as the centerpiece's base. Continuing with Max's memory of the coral, we wanted to stay fairly monochromatic, so we used real white coral placed in an urn and around the base and a coral-colored "coral," which, in fact, was also bought at a craft store and was made of rubber. Unless you actually touched it, you would never know it wasn't real. The rubber coral was supported by the other objects while the white coral assisted us later in being able to support the flowers we would add.

It seems that the stars—or should I say, fish—were aligned for us. Eva loves water elements, and she had a wonderful collection of seashells that she had gathered from all over the world. Coincidentally, the colors of the seashells matched our scheme with tones of white, silver, browns, beiges, and some orange-coral accents. These were just some of the elements that were already in her home that we were able to use. Remember when designing for any party, particularly a smaller dinner party, it is fun to see what's around the house to use as part of your decor and design. I actually do this on a regular basis!

Other objects that were lying around Eva's home were old books, which helped create the old-world feel we ended up with. We used the books to add height to the classic silver candlesticks, which we also found around the house. Dried coral around the candles gave an organic feel and also served as a scrim for the candlelight to travel through.

We also added beautiful cut-crystal candleholders as a glamorous boost. Having these smaller candleholders allowed us to control where and how we could use the candlelight since these could easily be placed throughout the arrangement. Miscellaneous elements like decorative glass balls came as an impromptu choice and added whimsy, creativity, and balance to the arrangement. Any decorative elements we used for the centerpiece that we couldn't find around Eva's home, we purchased at a craft store and spent less than one hundred dollars.

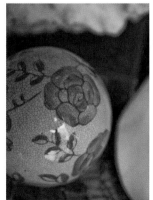

beginning the table setup

Once the initial centerpiece was completed, we brought all of our tabletop elements onto the table from the living room. The china Max chose was Vera Wang's Capri collection, which she designed for Wedgwood. I gave Max several options to choose from, and he said that these spoke to him most because of their white-and-coral color and because the plates actually reminded him of life preservers! They were absolutely perfect!

The accompanying flatware we used was Padova by Waterford. It was simple and elegant, but not over-the-top. The flatware had ridges, which made it very easy and comfortable to hold and maneuver.

Finally, the crystal had finished being washed and I brought the wineglasses and water goblets to the table as well so that we could take inventory of all items before we set the table.

We purposely set the table after the initial centerpiece was done but before adding the flowers and other elements because we wanted to make sure that we had room for the table settings. We decided not to use place mats to balance the complexity of the centerpiece while at the same time exposing the beautiful antiqued mirrored-glass top and dark wood table. Risky? Perhaps a bit, but we were expecting a sophisticated group of guests, who would be drinking only wine as an alcoholic beverage, so we didn't feel that people would get messy. I set the table by walking around it and starting with the dishes, eventually making several trips around the table before it was finally set.

I set the dinner plates with the lines going straight up and down, vertical and horizontal, and then we set the salad plates on top with the lines at angles. These plates really did look like life preservers, but elegant ones! Once the glasses were all placed, we could see exactly how much room would be left on the table.

napkins and place settings

Max and I created a wonderful and easy design for our napkin holders and place settings with names. Here are all the elements. These are easy steps you can do yourself!

NAPKINS
elements:

Cloth Napkins

Decorative Ribbon

Long Necklaces

Decorative Insert (Coral)

5 steps:

1. Fold your napkin diagonally in half to form a triangle and then fold the sides up to form a square.
2. Wrap your decorative ribbon around the folded napkin and tie a bow so that the open ends are on top.
3. Tie your necklace around the ribbon and napkin and secure it by tying it like a bow as well.
4. Tuck your decorative element inside the open napkin.
5. Cut the loose ends of the ribbon for a clean look.

Napkin Completed!

After we finished the napkins, we tried putting on the salad plates real dried starfish, which we would offer to our guests to take home, and then placed the napkins on top of the starfish.

We loved the way it looked, so while Max found all of the starfish and got the flowers ready to add to the table, I carefully pleated the drapes we had hung earlier in the day to get the room ready for the chairs to come in.

PLACE SETTINGS

elements: for makin...

Decorative Paper ...

Arts and Crafts Gl...

Decorative "Them...

Decal Lettering or...

Decorative Sticker...

5 easy steps:

1. Cut decorative ...
2. Fold the paper ...
   than the other. ...
3. Glue the decor...
   with the shorte...
4. Apply lettering ...
5. Add stickers w...

When finished, pu...
guests to sit. Remem...
didn't know one and ...
where people know ...
where everyone is go...
process less awkwar...

DETAILS, SPECIAL FEATURES, AND GUEST GIFTS

invitation and menu design

I talked to Keisha Beane, our invitation and menu designer, a lot about the dinner we had at Max's villa in Florence. I showed her pictures and told her related stories, because I really wanted her to understand just how beautiful and intimate that gathering was, even though it was set outdoors with a very long table for fifteen people.

For this Classic Dinner Party, I loved the idea of using a wax seal with an "X" stamp (of course) and fine paper to convey the chic style that our guests would encounter. The tone is set with the invitations, so I wanted to convey a really elegant time was to be had by all.

The invitation was made with a soft white paper, which we layered on top of a handmade paper that had a small amount of translucence to it. Keisha drew a beautiful piece of coral that resembled a sculpture by using ebony pencils and filling it in with red to resemble the coral that was used as a main focal point in the centerpiece.

The invitation was sealed with a wax stamp using the historic application style of melting wax and pressing the metal seal into it. The menu was made using the same techniques and adding embossed gold coral.

gifts

We used many of the decor elements as gifts for the guests. Although we had found Eva's seashell collection to use in the centerpiece, we purchased more shells at the arts-and-crafts store to sprinkle around the table to stimulate our guests' sense of touch and then also to take home as one of the gifts.

Each guest would also get a small fishbowl with a Chinese fighting fish swimming inside. The funny thing is that these fish are remarkably still when left alone. They are beautiful in color and added a magical and visually stimulating palette to our table. We placed the bowls on the bread plates before the guests' arrivals.

As an added treat, we bought two sets of tickets for two people to attend a local aquarium. We would raffle these tickets off at the end of the night. We used the guests' name tags and put them in a large bag and then pulled two out to find out who the winners were. The tickets were placed in an envelope that was decorated to match the place settings. One of the great things about having a raffle like this is that it marks the climax of the event and the end of the evening, and allows the host to decide when to let the guests feel comfortable about leaving.

Probably the most classy, interesting, and surprising gift was the pillow that would be placed on each of the guests' chairs. They were off-white linen pillows with coral embroidery. This was, after all, the premise for the design of the entire event.

SOUND | easy listening

FOR THE CLASSIC Dinner Party, I chose three songs that would be easy to listen to while a sit-down dinner was going on. The first, "Camelia," is a ballad in the classic standard style sung beautifully by Liela Avila.

The second song—from my 1993 solo project, *La Pasion*—is entitled "*Solamente Tu Me Llenas*," which means "only you make my life full." It's a Latin jazz-flavored song that I thought would work well for this party.

The third track is an instrumental jazz piece called "Brief Encounter" performed by the Blue Note Swing Orchestra. It's a smooth and elegant track that will put everyone in the mood to enjoy the party's food and wine!

TOUCH AND SMELL | wispy and exotic

FOR OUR CLASSIC Dinner Party, the flowers really ended up being a secondary accessory. We chose fresh stems of ginger, curly willow, palm leaves, and orchids, as well as a few other exotics.

We carefully inserted the longer stems of flowers into the centerpiece where there was an available opening that would also support the stem. These are hardy flowers, so we weren't forced to worry about water for them.

The white coral was the perfect place for us to place individual orchids at the lower level of the centerpiece for balance. The coral solidly held the orchid in place. Once we had our color in, we added green ginger leaves and palm leaves to finish off the arrangement.

One of my acquaintances, Joe Rowe, is a florist in Los Angeles. He found out the theme of the evening and put together a small arrangement as a gift! It was a beautiful arrangement of tightly packed white roses, orchids, and hydrangeas in a glass vase with seashells at the bottom. Our table was complete, so we couldn't use it there, but we did decide to use it at the appetizer and wine station instead. Bringing flowers to a dinner party as a gift is a great thing to do!

ready for our guests!

Our preparations were complete, and there was just enough space on the table for all of our elements to work together. The final product was a beautiful example of taking a small and specific element, the coral, and allowing ourselves to run wild with creativity. We were ready to receive our guests with a little time to spare to have a glass of wine, celebrate, and enjoy our work.

TASTE surf and turf

To Start

roasted bosc pear and roquefort salad

•

Proceed with

easy tuna tartare with sweet chili and avocado

•

Followed by

surf and turf of shrimp and crawfish with pepper-thyme-
crusted filet of beef and easy red wine sauce

•

To Accompany

creamy white polenta and grilled haricot vert

(french green beans)

•

Dessert

warm pear crumble à la mode

•

*Paired with

KIDS: cranberry cooler

classic martini with fresh stilton-stuffed olives

justin vineyards isosceles from paso robles, california

(a blend of 79% cabernet sauvignon,

11% cabernet franc, and 10% merlot)

ABOUT THE MENU

OUR EXECUTIVE CHEF and my collaborator in the kitchen, Ronnda Hamilton, is a well-known culinarian who has worked in some of the most prestigious restaurants in the United States and Europe. I feel very fortunate to have her as my guide into the world of delicious food.

For the Classic Dinner Party, Ronnda and I took a mini field trip to the market to search for the food that we wanted to serve. Ronnda opted for a specialty grocer that she knew had interesting fruits and vegetables, as well as the freshest meats and fish. I love going to boutique food stores. The colors and the smells are usually wonderfully overwhelming. With Ronnda, I was able to learn a lot about different items that I took for granted other than expecting them to taste really good!

roasted bosc pear and roquefort salad

We stopped in the fruit aisle, and Ronnda began telling me about Bosc pears and the fact that they are quite often overlooked in supermarkets. D'Anjou or Bartlett pears usually appear more appealing because of their inviting green skin. However, there is a delicious secret lurking behind the tan skin of the Bosc pear. THE SECRET: It is an elegant, mild pear flavor that shines in savory dishes like this salad. Bosc pears hold up to baking very well, and they make a beautiful plate presentation. The pear and Roquefort salad is a surefire crowd-pleaser for young and old alike, especially with the addition of pistachio nuts. Did you know that the pistachio is the official nut of classical French cuisine? I sure didn't. *Jeopardy!,* here I come. We continued the classic French theme with the addition of Roquefort, the French granddaddy of the current trend in blue cheese popularity.

easy tuna tartare
with sweet chili and avocado

Whenever I go to Japanese restaurants, I have to order tuna tartare. Tartare is a term used for raw meat seasoned and diced or ground into small pieces typically garnished with a raw egg. As we stopped by the fresh-seafood department, Ronnda told me that tartare's popularity originated in Hamburg, Germany, where the very first hamburgers were prepared in this style. Now the term is loosely translated to include vegetables, fish, and other items. Ronnda uses the tartare technique when she wants to highlight the natural flavor of extraordinary raw products. Its high-fashion originator, steak tartare, seems to have fallen from favor to make room for its lighter, healthier counterpart, tuna. Tuna tartare is a great conversation piece at dinner parties. There will usually be at least one guest trying this for the first time. You can make tartare from any of your favorite sushi fish. This Asian- inspired recipe will translate well. The great thing is the ease of this recipe compared to the gourmet value of it. People will think you are a culinary genius for coming up with this dish. Simply cut the tuna and avocado in advance, and add the marinade just before you serve it.

surf and turf of shrimp and crawfish with pepper-thyme-crusted filet of beef and easy red wine sauce

YUM! Surf and turf. I used to have that on special occasions when my family and I went out to dinner. It always seemed too decadent, but always delicious. Ronnda and I decided to come up with a great spin on surf and turf, where classic French meets classic American cuisine. While this dish may seem intimidating, Ronnda assured me that it is one of the easiest recipes in this book. If you have a business dinner or in-laws you need to impress, this menu is for you. The crawfish tails and shrimp are prepared like scampi. The creamy polenta takes ten minutes to prepare and can be done in advance and warmed up for your dinner, and the same goes for the petite French green beans. The magic, Ronnda insisted, is in the sauce. The sauce is actually a plain wine reduction, which means there is nothing added to the wine as it is reduced . . . where the excess wine slowly evaporates while the remaining wine thickens, intensifying the flavor of the sauce. We would suggest to choose a wine that is inexpensive but completely drinkable. It will make a better sauce than just wine labeled "cooking wine" and most important, you can have a glass while cooking under the guise of tasting for the recipe. Makes the cooking more fun in many cases.

creamy white polenta and grilled haricot vert (french green beans)

We definitely indulged with this dish. White polenta is Ronnda's favorite because she uses old-fashioned Southern grits, a dish she grew up with. Not having made grits before, although I've eaten them quite a bit, I wasn't sure how easy or hard they are to prepare. In actuality, they are really easy to make, and they are a great alternative to the same old mashed potatoes that are usually served with steak. Even though Ronnda's background is as a spa chef, which usually leads her down a road of lighter, healthier food—which I try to eat . . . but we all know it's hard to do consistently—we had some fun and made this polenta really decadent with lots of butter, cream, and aged Parmesan cheese. It will balance well with the butter-basted filet mignon. ENJOY!

THE RECIPES

roasted bosc pear and roquefort salad

1 tbsp butter

3 Bosc pears, cut in half

1 bag spring mixed greens

$\frac{1}{2}$ cup Roquefort blue cheese

1 cup caramelized pistachios

In a heavy baking dish, melt the butter and place the cut pears face-down. Roast in the oven for 30 minutes. Allow to cool. On a plate, arrange the mixed greens, blue cheese, and pistachios with the half-caramelized pears. Serve salad dressing on the side.

BALSAMIC VINEGAR SALAD DRESSING

1 cup aged balsamic vinegar

3 cups extra-virgin olive oil

salt

pepper

2 tbsp brown sugar

Combine all the ingredients in a blender and serve.

easy tuna tartare with sweet chili and avocado

1 lb fresh tuna steak, chopped into small cubes

1 shallot, chopped fine

1 avocado, cut into small cubes

6 sprigs chives, chopped

4 tbsp sesame oil

$\frac{1}{2}$ cup soy sauce

$\frac{1}{8}$ cup lemon juice

salt

$\frac{1}{2}$ cup sweet chili sauce

toasted sesame seeds

SERVES 6.

In a bowl combine the tuna, shallot, avocado, and chives. Mix well and refrigerate. Separately combine the sesame oil, soy sauce, lemon juice, and salt. Mix well and refrigerate. Just before serving, combine the marinade with the tuna mixture. Spoon 3 tablespoons of the tuna mixture into a ring mold. Top with the sweet chili sauce, and garnish with sesame seeds. Remove the ring mold and serve.

surf and turf of shrimp and crawfish with pepper-thyme-crusted filet of beef and easy red wine sauce

and

creamy white polenta and grilled haricot vert (french green beans)

3/4 cup olive oil

3 tbsp garlic, minced

1/2 lb medium shrimp, peeled and cleaned

1/2 lb crawfish tails, cleaned

salt

1 tbsp parsley, chopped

6 tsp fresh ground pepper

6 tsp fresh thyme leaves

6 8-oz filet mignon steaks

1 bottle red wine

1 box grits

2 cups heavy cream

1 cup shredded Gruyère or Parmesan cheese

1 lb French green beans (haricot vert), cleaned

Pour ¼ cup of the olive oil in a hot sauté pan, add 1 tablespoon minced garlic, the shrimp, and the crawfish tails. Cook until the shrimp are pink and cooked through. Season the mixture with salt, garnish with chopped parsley, and set aside.

Combine salt, pepper, and thyme leaves, and roll the steaks in the mixture on all sides. Prepare a hot sauté pan with ¼ cup of olive oil. Sear the steaks on all sides until medium-rare. Meanwhile in a pot, bring the bottle of wine to a boil and simmer until the wine is reduced to ¼ its original amount.

Prepare 6 to 8 portions of quick grits according to instructions on the box. When the grits are done, stir in 1 tablespoon minced garlic, the heavy cream, the cheese, and salt, to taste.

Bring 2 quarts water to a boil and add the green beans. Cook for approximately 8 minutes or until the beans are slightly tender. Remove from boiling water and submerge in cold water. Set aside and toss with salt to taste and ¼ cup olive oil.

On a plate place some hot green beans, creamy polenta, and a steak. Top the steak with shrimp mixture and serve the red wine sauce on the side.

warm pear crumble à la mode

6 D'Anjou pears, cored and cut into wedges

1 cup brown sugar

$\frac{1}{4}$ cup lemon juice

2 tbsp ground cinnamon

1 tbsp vanilla extract

1 tbsp almond extract

$\frac{1}{4}$ cup white raisins

1 stick butter, cut into small pieces

topping

2 cups whole oats

1 cup melted butter

1 tsp ground cinnamon

$\frac{1}{2}$ cup brown sugar

premium ice cream

SERVES 6.

In a bowl combine the pears, sugar, lemon juice, cinnamon, vanilla, almond extract, and white raisins. Toss well and pour into a baking dish. Top with the butter pieces. Separately, in a bowl, combine the items for topping and mix well. Pour the topping over the pears, and bake at 350°F for 1 hour. Serve warm and top with your favorite premium ice cream.

classic martini with fresh stilton-stuffed olives

vermouth
premium vodka or gin
large green-pitted olives
1 small wedge Stilton cheese

Break the Stilton into small pieces. Stuff the Stilton into cavities of
the pitted olives. Refrigerate until you are ready to use them. Rinse
a chilled martini glass with vermouth. Fill the glass with vodka, and
garnish it with stuffed olives.

cranberry cooler

1 bottle cranberry juice cocktail
1 bottle ginger ale
lime wedges

Fill a tall glass with ice. Pour 3 parts ginger ale to 1 part cranberry
juice. Squeeze the juice from 1 lime wedge into the glass and garnish
it with the lime wedge. (This drink is perfect for kids.)

RECAP

THE SPACE LOOKED magnificent, and as I took a look at the table in the mirror, I felt as if it was another world filled with fantasy and wonder. This would be a truly amazing dinner party.

Max shared with me a quote from his father, who said, "You should never have your guests forget the dinner party you threw. It should be talked about for at least six months afterward." I have a feeling that because of this book, we will fulfill his advice! Don't forget this! After all, it is one of Max's family secrets in entertaining that I'm sharing with you!

CLASSIC DINNER PARTY TIPS

1. Try to keep your dinner party guest count to a maximum of ten to twelve. More than a dozen people makes it difficult to do table service efficiently.

2. Make the theme work with the setting. Use the room as a guide to the rest of your design.

3. Try to keep your design budget inexpensive by being very creative. Set your amount ahead of time.

4. Make many of your design elements gifts! This way you get more bang for your buck.

5. Choose music that will work well for background so that it doesn't disturb conversation at the table.

6. Stay with only wine and champagne as your only alcoholic beverages. In an intimate setting, wine is more conducive to conversations.

courses is something different and easy to do. Laying out a pathway of rose petals gives a visual imprint to the party and smells great.

Over the years, I have found that even if people are not designers themselves and don't have the so-called "design gene," they still very much appreciate a beautiful presentation. To be sure, there is nothing subtle about the design and decorations of this Princess Party. But isn't that the point, really? This is a party for a young woman who is entering adulthood, wanting to make her own statement, but still keeping in mind she and her friends want to have fun. You'll notice as you turn the pages that in addition to the guest of honor, this party is all about the tables and, in particular, the tabletops. The design and decorations are not only a bit whimsical, but, in all honesty, sophisticated, tasteful, and elegant.

VISION | playful and regal

table and party setup

There was no shortage of objects to touch, smell, and interact with. A number of small items was added, such as porcelain shoes that could double as cell phone holders; topiaries in the shapes of purses and stilettos; iridescent marbles that shimmered in the sun; faux crystal lipstick cases that were actually pens; and cute luggage tags in the shape of shoes, on which guests' names could be placed.

Overall it was important that the decorations looked organic in nature, where it seemed things were put here and there in a coordinated fashion, but

not stiff or staged. I believe this was accomplished, but I have to say that every placement—whether it was the flowers, marbles, flower petals, glassware, or jewelry—was specifically placed in such a fashion that each guest was able to see something slightly different than her table mates. We tried several different variations before we were happy with the results. So don't be nervous to try various looks. When it is right, it will shine and you will know it. We actually had fun laying everything out, since we had such latitude, given the pieces we were decorating with. There were truly no right and wrong.

As we showcase these events, we are inviting you to step out of your comfort zone and to do things that are a bit daring. If hot pink and variations thereof are not for you, choose colors that you and the young woman are comfortable with. If you are more into earth tones and neutrals, that is fine, but I would urge you to spice it up with the unexpected. That is where you will get your "wow" factor. It will also set the tone of the party. For this Princess Party, invitees will know from the get-go that this will not be a quiet event. Instead, fun will be had, and many surprises will be in store.

As you can see, there were a lot of pinks and purples to play with. Marley, with Ursula, a floral designer, in the background, is putting together and laying out the arrangements and settings on the table. The yard in this case was quite large, so we had to be careful that the nine tables didn't get lost or look too small in comparison. We decided to keep the tables closely aligned with one another, in the hope that this would inspire guests to get up and mingle. Further, we assumed that guests at a Princess Party would want to be near one another. We purposely placed the bar in a corner of the property. We wanted to avoid a bottleneck that could impinge on the comfort of the other guests, should lines form. If we had worked with a smaller area or had set up the party inside, I would have suggested that a bar area be placed away from the main sitting area. A line of people snaking through the tables just to get a drink could very quickly make for a forgettable party. A guest bedroom or den could easily be made over to house a bartender or a "do it yourself" beverage stand. The kitchen would be the most logical place for a bar, but nine times out of ten, there will be a lot of activity in the kitchen already with appetizers and main courses coming in and out.

The bar was indeed set up away from the main seating area, yet it was connected to the whole by using the pink linen and other elements that were used throughout the party. However, with that said, the decor on the bar was not a bigger version of what was on the other tables. Further, the wire-frame mannequins with the cocktail dresses were made specifically for the party, and they were completely different from anything on the nine other tables. The girlie tulle fabric and the use of candy as a design element on the dresses made for an unexpected and visually stunning display. It was also another concept for people to look at, touch, comment on, talk about, and have fun with.

The white dress pulled from the white china dishes with gold rims while the large glass vases, which were not used in the main seating area, tied in the crystal glasses that were on the tables. Jewels in the floral display mirrored the decor on the tabletops, and the strewn petals were closely aligned to the pathway on the grass. Why go to all of this trouble and not make the bar simple and plain?

The flower arrangement at one end of the bar is among my favorites. I love how there are several jewels just floating about the arrangement, seemingly suspended as if they are waiting for someone to notice them. Who wouldn't notice this display? A tiara and a wand are lying on top of hydrangeas and other beautiful flowers. If there was a flat surface anywhere to be found, we put some outrageously fun decor on top of it. If it gets the guests walking, talking, and having fun, I am all for it.

chairs

We chose simple black wood chairs for several reasons.

1. One of the first ideas we came up with was to have Chiavari chairs, which are classically elegant chairs with gently sloping backs with a bamboo design. We thought to possibly drape them in some dramatic fashion, but in the end, we felt that these chairs would take away from the throne chair, which is a main focal point of the party.

2. Upholstered chairs might end up getting dirty, especially during setup in the morning when the ground is moist with dew. The potential of having to pay extra for cleaning upon returning them to the rental shop was something we didn't want to add into our budget.

3. The black chairs we decided on were beautifully aesthetic and deceptively simple in design. They complemented the tabletop without taking away from the decorations. They also tied into the black mesh used in the topiaries found on the tabletops.

4. They are easily stored and not heavy to carry.

5. In terms of budgetary concerns, these folding chairs are much less costly than Chiavari or upholstered chairs would have cost. Believe me, we looked at chairs with some absolutely exquisite fabric, but the cost wasn't justifiable.

6. If I can leave you with one thought, you don't want to rent just

any chair. It has to be a purposeful decision that ties into the whole event. You don't want it to look like you ran out of money and got any old chair you found.

The throne was a fun addition to the Princess Party and very integral to the overall design of the party. The guests wouldn't necessarily realize it, but the throne ties into the gold of the flatware, dishes, and crystal. It is unifying and neatly packages many of the design elements.

Everyone knows that a princess needs a throne to sit on while talking to her subjects—er—guests. In this case, the heavily carved gilt wood chair sporting a crest, powerful lion heads, and purple velour fabric, screamed royalty. Any young woman sitting on this chair will feel like the center of the universe. The throne also served as a great way to get kids and adults alike to sit for pictures. It turns out everyone wants to be the prince and princess of the ball.

Since the tablescapes were our canvas with which to work, we wanted the tables to be a feast for the eyes. These 48-inch square tables seat eight comfortably. This configuration was decided upon since long tables don't give a chance for people to talk to one another easily. I also think they are a bit overwhelming for teenagers. We wanted a more relaxed environment where the guests could mingle with one another easily.

environment

This party was being held outdoors in a beautifully landscaped yard, and because of that, it was important for the decor to hold up well against the gardens that surrounded it.

It was also important to make the yard fresh and new, creating a different perspective for people who might have been here many times prior. The furniture and color palette needed to stand out and speak for itself. In this case, hot pinks and soft variations of pink did the trick. Hot colors such as pinks and lime greens and bright yellows can be amazing to work with, but they need to be toned down with complementary soft colors. If you don't tone them down, you might end up in a 1960s psychedelic hole, and these hot colors will show deficiencies in the design if there is nothing to counterbalance them. In this case, the hot pinks were tempered by various shades of pink and, to a lesser degree, white.

For a brief moment we thought about having this Princess Party inside the house. It would have been less expensive to throw, since the number of tables that could have fit inside was quite small. This would have meant cutting down the guest list, the food and beverage requirements, and the staffing needs. Of course, it could have been done and would have been beautiful, but we wanted to take advantage of an outdoor space where people were able to mingle and roam around freely from table to table. Also, events thrown outdoors seem to be more carefree and joyous, and I have no doubt guests can definitely sense it. While an outdoor soiree might have the same formalities as one that might be held in a hall or home, they do tend to be less reserved. On the other hand, throwing a party outside is tricky. You have to count on the weather being nice, the neighbors not mowing their lawns, and guests not being allergic to various pollens and mosses. Personally, I love throwing outdoor festivities. The fresh air, the sound of birds, the smell of flowers, and the hypnotic sway of the trees are all truly relaxing to me. I also believe people are happier in the fresh air and are more likely to sit longer and meet new people. Thankfully, the day this party was thrown, the sky was a brilliant blue and the birds were chirping away, providing a beautiful sonic soundscape for our event.

place setting and table setting ideas

Gold-plated cutlery has limitations—we all know that. But for a Princess Party, we thought that gold was truly the way to go. It actually set a very opulent tone. The raised-vine-and-floral designs on the plate's rim were beautiful and actually cool to touch. As a kid, I always played with the raised

surfaces on plates. I don't know why. It probably gave me something to do, but it stuck in my mind that people do look at dishes, usually turning them over to see where they came from.

The dishes, serving pieces, and glassware were all coordinated. Again, there is a theme, a complementary style, and an overall plan of action. Seen through to its conclusion, the tables are a sparkling reminder of how color, texture, and fragrance can work magic.

If, for example, you wanted to use your mother's and grandmother's china, where different styles of plates would intermingle on the tabletops, the centerpieces would have to be homogenized and toned down since the heirloom china is the new focal point. Instead of unreserved floral displays, the Dupioni silk box would have sported a tamed bouquet of roses with the butterfly attached to one of the sides. I would have kept the crystal glasses with the gold rim as well as the gold-plated cutlery to tie into the throne, but instead of the pink napkin, I would have taken the opportunity to place a striking gold lamé napkin (metallic sheen) that would stand out.

DETAILS, SPECIAL FEATURES, AND GUEST GIFTS

invitation and menu design

A common thread of all the designs you will see in the "Invitations and Menus" section of each chapter is the fact that we want to encourage interaction with you, the reader, and push the three-dimensional characteristics of each invitation. We were also keenly aware of the fact that we wanted people to have the confidence to go out and try to create their own invitations and menus. You know the theme of your party, the colors you want to use, and the food that you will be serving. So why not give it a try? Your guests will be impressed and your invitation will certainly be one of a kind!

With that said, for the Princess Party, we wanted to create a fun, sophisticated, and "girlie" invitation. Keisha came up with the idea of designing a purse that is decked out in rhinestones and colored in bright colors, which, by the way, match our color palette. Right away, the recipient knows that this is going to be a loud and festive event.

Keisha used hand-printed paper with rhinestone detailing for decoration and to create a clasplike effect. In essence, you would be able to open the purse and have the contents of a party inside, or in this case the who, what, where, and the when.

As for the menu, we wanted it to have a similar sparkle. So the wrapped present or a hatbox look was created to allow for the idea that surprises (the unexpected and delicious food choices) are in store and all tied up with a bow.

centerpiece

Okay, forget the pink theme. We are talking shoes, shoes, shoes. I admit it!! What young woman doesn't like shoes?! In this case we found some great topiaries in the shape of wickedly high-heeled stilettos and proceeded to decorate them with roses. Looking closely you can see crystal-shaped diamonds that were placed in the center of the rosebuds to give them a luxurious touch.

You can easily make any pair of shoes into a centerpiece. Thrift stores and charitable organizations usually have any number of used shoes to choose from, and they are, for the most part, inexpensive and come in pairs! More bang for a buck or two! I would have no problem placing some cool old pair of shoes in the middle of a fancy table if I thought I could create something special out of them. It's like looking at a home that needs fixing. Are the bones good? Can you work with it? Rehab it? Patent leather shoes with buckles or a strappy high-heeled number can be the start of some truly liberating and inspiring design.

In addition to the faux diamonds, we liberally placed shimmering glass marbles within the flower petals. People will look once and have to look a second time to see what they actually are. It is easy, cheap, and fun to do. Bottom line, there are any number of things that can be used that won't take up too much room on a table and that can create great conversation. By the way, your friends will think you're a genius!

gifts

Your friends and family will also think you're generous if you find some colorful and different accessories that could be well used for guest gifts. These glazed clay shoes can be used as cell phone holders, place-card holders, or paperweights. The luggage tags can double as seat holders and, as well, luggage tags. I hate to have party favors that I believe are just going to be thrown away. The fun purple bejeweled lipstick case is actually a pen, and the shoe is a delicious cookie in frosted pinks. We tried to come up with a number of innovative giveaways to make for a memorable day. If you don't want guests to think that everything on the table is up for grabs, make an announcement that under one or three or five seats is a pink sticker, and if your chair has one of these stickers, you get to take whatever the sticker says on it. I guarantee you that everyone will be flipping those chairs over!

SOUND | youthful and fun

FOR THE PRINCESS Party, I wanted to choose songs that were youthful and fun. The first song, "Fanfare to a Princess," I actually wrote for my sister's wedding as her wedding march. She wanted to be princess for a day, so she wore a veil with a tiara. I also composed a series of songs with that theme for the ceremony. I think this song works well as a presentation or entrance song for the girl celebrating her fifteenth, sixteenth, or seventeenth birthday!

The second song, "Yearbook," performed by Katlin Rivers, is a song about a young girl recollecting the immediate past and the fun she has had with her friends. It is really uplifting, and the sound is very current for our young princesses.

The third song, "Happy," is just that: a happy song! It's performed by Caitlin Crosby, and the style is similar to the previous song, which makes this selection very cohesive.

TOUCH AND SMELL | jewels and pink flowers

NOT ONLY WAS there a spread of smooth and textured objects and items to touch, but the aromatic pink floral pieces set the delightful mood for such a playful event. Also, the floral pieces, while plentiful, were not tall in stature. This was purposely done so as not to block one guest from another on the opposite side of the table; otherwise it would most certainly inhibit conversation. There is nothing more annoying to me than having two people trying to talk to each other with a huge plant separating them, making it hard to see across a table. Most of the time, people will just give up and talk to their immediate neighbors to their left or right. Thus, taking into account the scale of the table is very important. These tables are not large by any means, so you shouldn't have pieces that alone cover a large swath of the table. Visually it will throw everything off and look unbalanced.

In these two photos you will notice a slightly different view of the same table. Each side has something different to look at. It is fun for the guests because a game of musical chairs will no doubt ensue when they realize there are a lot of things to see on the table. It will assist in breaking the ice among people who don't know one another and will hopefully foster table-wide conversations.

Marley likes to use the word "unexpected" a lot, and I absolutely agree with her. It is important to create an atmosphere of, well, surprises. Take the pink candles for example. Lit candles in broad daylight? Obviously we didn't need them to see with, but they certainly make the table more interesting to look at. To put it simply, why not have candles? When you get thank-you cards from guests writing you about how much they loved the party and commenting on all of the surprises, it will make it all worthwhile.

As we went along, there was a distinct possibility that the tables were becoming too crowded, too heavy and overburdened with flowers, jewelry, and other accessories. We still had to leave room for the plates and serving utensils, elements that were just as important to the overall look. By no means should the dishes be an afterthought in the overall look of the party. It is easy to get simple, ordinary plates and move on, but that would be a mistake. If the dishes don't complement or add to the theme, which is your common thread, your unifying qualities will be lost. In the end, we did take off one small arrangement from the table, but otherwise, we decided to keep the table chock-full of all sorts of unexpected surprises.

For the centerpieces, we decided on Dupioni silk–wrapped boxes, which we had custom-made. We spent more money on these than we had originally planned to, but at the same time we were proportioning where to put the money. We rented inexpensive poly-cotton standard linens for the tables and less expensive folding chairs. Neither of these elements looked cheap or out of place. The Dupioni silk box surrounded simple glass vases that fit

neatly inside. I love this wrapped box idea because it is something almost anyone can execute. Wallpaper, wrapping paper, or other fabric could have just as easily been used in place of the silk. It is a fun and inexpensive project to make. The newly formed surround gives added texture to an otherwise flat surface, while creating a little piece of art in its own right.

As an alternative to floral displays, you could very easily create a novel centerpiece using clear glass urns that are full to the rim with candies. One table could have a red vine bouquet with a great girlie bow around it. Another centerpiece can be a beautiful arrangement of large pink-colored lollipops, while a third could have pink-and-white cupcakes on sticks that are tied

together with cotton candy. Because each table has a different candy display, guests will definitely be moving around to inspect them, and should they be part of the giveaways, everyone will want them!

In this particular case, the flowers were chosen because they were bold in color, soft in touch, fragrant, and beautiful. The dahlias, hydrangeas, and roses make a dramatic impression upon first glance. These flowers are loud and proud; they want to be noticed. Again, this works because there is nothing subtle about the design. It is fantastical, inspiring, and fun.

The jeweled butterflies add a bit of whimsical charm. They look like they could have just landed on the table, making their way to the fresh-cut flowers. We also spread rose petals on the table, knowing that guests would hold them to their noses to smell. This does two things. First, some of the fragrance will come off on their hands, allowing people to carry the scent for a while. Second, while not scientific by any means, I've noticed that a person's demeanor is vastly improved when she is in contact with flowers. The fragrant smell of fresh-cut flowers visibly relaxes people. I think it is because it brings them closer to nature. It might also trigger a fond memory that reminds them of a childhood garden or a great weekend away. Whatever it is, flowers always make a party better!

The purse-shaped topiary is a fun and creative addition to the table. We placed large colored-glass diamonds and rubies inside the purse to give it a magical, old-world feeling while maintaining a contemporary twenty-first-century twist.

As you might have noticed, the floral arrangements are key to the design of the Princess Party. In the upper-left photo the roses, hydrangeas, and dahlias are used as a pedestal to showcase a drop-dead-gorgeous faux-diamond tennis bracelet. Again, this was an unexpected and creative way to incorporate several different elements without straying from our central theme. The glass bowl actually had sentimental value and was a nice way to use a family heirloom to bring back happy memories.

One meeting we had dealt entirely with the type of pathway we should put down that leads the princess to her party. A red carpet with paparazzi taking pictures? A pink faux-fur runner? In the end we decided on this lovely trail of rose petals. It was as if we perfumed the area with a spray. It was magical and very princess-like.

TASTE | gourmet classics

To Start

petite smoked chicken quesadillas with avocado salsa

•

Proceed with

lump crab martini with citrus and candied kumquats

•

Followed by

mini kobe burgers

with grilled red onions and aged cheddar

•

To Accompany

mini gourmet hot dogs with exotic relishes

•

Dessert

assorted cupcakes:

lemon, ginger, chocolate, and pistachio

&

trio of sweet and savory popcorns

(maple rosemary and parmesan olive oil)

•

*Paired with

shirley temple with gin

KIDS: fresh ginger ale

ABOUT THE MENU

THE MENU SHOULD be fun and whimsically suitable for a young girl, but with a gourmet touch to keep its formality. Ronnda put together a menu that is chic, fun, and delicious!

gourmet mini hot dogs with exotic relishes

For the mini gourmet hot dogs, search out your city's best sausage maker. Set aside time to go in and purchase one of each of his most interesting flavors and one safe flavor. Go home and taste away. Make a tally of the best qualities of each and make your selection. Now for the bread. Ronnda loves serving these little tasties on the crustiest baguettes she can find. Purchase the thinner baguettes to avoid them getting too bready for the sausages.

For both Ronnda and me, sampling is our favorite part of making a menu. I call it the party before the storm. The really fun part of these little dogs is the relishes. Here's your chance to include a piece of your heritage in the party. Make a relish or two from cultural ingredients. For example add peppers and onions for an Italian flair. Try wasabi mustard for a Japanese touch or a spicy avocado salsa for a Latin flavor.

mini kobe burgers with grilled red onions and aged cheddar

Everybody, no matter how picky, loves a good hamburger. The new breed of upscale burgers served at high-end restaurants has made the hamburger a chic accessory to a formal party menu, and Ronnda feels that there is no more decadent choice of meat on the market than fresh-ground Kobe Beef. You will be elevated to superstar status by the true carnivores in your group. The famous Kobe style of raising cows originated in Japan, with a select group of young cows raised like royalty. Australians and Americans now raise beef in this Kobe style at a fraction of the cost while maintaining the flashy name that is sure to garner lots of *oohs* and *aahs*! Be sure to check your calorie count at the door; this beef has almost twice the amount of marbling as regular beef. Combine this with the decadently prepared grilled onions and a high-quality aged cheddar. It's a good thing these burgers are mini.

lump crab martini with citrus and candied kumquats

How can you go wrong with this lovely sweet crab in a martini glass? In the interest of time, Ronnda recommends purchasing fresh crabmeat already picked from the shell instead of buying whole crabs and preparing them yourself. The great thing about buying crab already picked is that you can choose the crab you want according to your flavor preferences and budget. The most affordable type of crab is meat from the claw of the crab. It is not quite as sweet and has a bit of a salty flavor. It is great if you have a dish that may mask some of the flavor of the crab with other ingredients. In that case, it does not really make sense to spend a lot of money on flavorful crab that you may not taste very much in the dish. For this reason you may find claw meat used in many restaurants for everything from crab artichoke dip to crab quesadillas and enchiladas. The middle-priced option of crab is called back fin. It has a less salty flavor and is sweeter than claw meat. It's a nice middle-grade option. Many people will be perfectly satisfied with its flavor profile. This is the crab that you may receive in most high-end restaurants unless they specify otherwise. In the restaurant business, it's called special crab. The highest grade of crab is called lump. It is large chunks of very sweet crab with a nice mild flavor, not salty. Ronnda highly recommends this crab for your martini, but lump crab can be really expensive, and if you are feeding a large group, you may opt for special or back-fin crab

and be completely satisfied with it, and your guests will be none the wiser. It is very important to keep crab refrigerated at all times. It can spoil very quickly. Purchase it from a reputable market, be sure to check the expiration date, and ask when the crab came into the market to make sure it is fresh. Kumquats make this dish really fun and give guests a little to talk about, especially around holiday time. I grew up with a kumquat tree outside of my kitchen. I love them. If you can't find kumquats for this dish, you may substitute orange zest. If you start with this fresh sweet crab, this dish will hit a home run with guests every time.

trio of sweet and savory popcorns
like maple rosemary and parmesan olive oil

What better way to end a party than with popcorn? Add an elegant touch with provincial French and Tuscan flavors. Remember to use the freshest herbs you can find, real maple syrup, and properly aged Parmesan. This whimsical, easy dish will be enjoyed equally by adults and hard-to-please teens.

THE RECIPES

trio of sweet and savory popcorn: maple rosemary and parmesan olive oil

2 sticks butter, melted

1/2 cup olive oil

salt, to taste

1 box microwave popcorn

1/4 cup maple syrup

2 tbsp fresh rosemary, chopped

1/2 cup Parmesan, grated

1 orange, zest only

2 tsp fresh lavender flowers

Melt the butter and combine with the olive oil and salt to taste. Pop the microwave popcorn according to box instructions. Divide the popcorn and butter-oil mixture into 3 equal portions. Add the maple syrup and rosemary to the first batch of butter, and toss it with 1 portion of the popcorn. Add the second batch of butter and Parmesan cheese to the second portion of popcorn, and toss well. Add orange zest to the remaining butter and pour it over the third batch of popcorn. Garnish with lavender flowers.

lump crab martini
with citrus and candied kumquats

1 lb lump crab

1 red bell pepper, diced small

1 shallot, diced small

1 lemon, juice and zest

6 chives, chopped

SERVES 6.

Toss all the ingredients together. Add sliced candied kumquat, per the recipe below. Spoon into chilled martini glasses. Garnish with whole candied kumquats.

CANDIED KUMQUATS

1 cup sugar

$\frac{1}{2}$ cup water

kumquats

Combine sugar and water in a pot and bring to a boil. Add the kumquats. Cook for 30 seconds. Then place the kumquats on a cookie sheet and allow them to cool.

petite smoked chicken quesadillas
with avocado salsa

2-lb smoked chicken, cut in $\frac{1}{4}$-inch slabs

$\frac{1}{4}$ cup olive oil

1 onion, diced small

lump crab martini
with citrus and candied kumquats

1 lb lump crab

1 red bell pepper, diced small

1 shallot, diced small

1 lemon, juice and zest

6 chives, chopped

SERVES 6.

Toss all the ingredients together. Add sliced candied kumquat, per the recipe below. Spoon into chilled martini glasses. Garnish with whole candied kumquats.

CANDIED KUMQUATS

1 cup sugar

1/2 cup water

kumquats

Combine sugar and water in a pot and bring to a boil. Add the kumquats. Cook for 30 seconds. Then place the kumquats on a cookie sheet and allow them to cool.

petite smoked chicken quesadillas
with avocado salsa

2-lb smoked chicken, cut in 1/4-inch slabs

1/4 cup olive oil

1 onion, diced small

mini kobe burgers
with grilled red onions and aged cheddar

1 lb ground Kobe beef (substitute ground sirloin if needed)

1 onion, diced

2 tbsp butter, melted

2 tbsp olive oil

2 tbsp fresh thyme

5 cloves garlic, chopped

1 red onion, julienned

1 cup red wine

1 tbsp sugar

mini brioche rolls or small sweet dinner rolls

6 slices aged Cheddar cheese, cut in half

Combine the Kobe beef, diced onions, melted butter, 1 tablespoon of olive oil, thyme, and garlic in a bowl, and mix well. Cover and refrigerate for 15 minutes. Meanwhile, sauté the red onions in 1 tablespoon of olive oil until translucent. Then add the red wine and sugar. Simmer for 20 minutes, remove from fire, and set aside. While onions are caramelizing, get the Kobe beef mixture from refrigerator. Form patties with 2 tablespoons of Kobe beef mixture, and fry on a hot pan to desired temperature (medium-rare or well-done). Cut the rolls in half and toast on a hot pan or in a toaster oven. Assemble burgers with 1 patty, 1 slice Cheddar, and 1 teaspoon caramelized onions. Top with other half of the roll. Use a frilly toothpick to hold the burgers together. Serve hot.

mini gourmet hot dogs with exotic relish

1 stick butter

2 thin baguettes or crusty rolls, cut into 2-inch pieces

assorted sausages or your favorite wieners, cut into 2-inch pieces

2 tsp olive oil

2 red bell peppers, julienned

2 onions, julienned

1 tsp fresh thyme leaves

1 cup white wine

2 cups Dijon mustard

Spread the butter into the centers of the baguettes and lightly toast them on a flat grill. Boil the sausage sections in hot water, and remove them when plump and cooked on the inside. In a sauté pan, add 1 teaspoon of the olive oil; then combine the peppers and 1 onion. Cook until both are limp and translucent. Separately, sauté 1 onion, 1 teaspoon olive oil, and the thyme together in a sauté pan until the onions are translucent. In a small pot, bring the white wine to a boil. Add the mustard and simmer for 15 minutes.

Before serving, put the meat on baguettes. Set out the peppers, thyme, onions, and white wine mustard in small bowls surrounding a platter of sandwiches.

THE RECIPES

trio of sweet and savory popcorn: maple rosemary and parmesan olive oil

2 sticks butter, melted

$\frac{1}{2}$ cup olive oil

salt, to taste

1 box microwave popcorn

$\frac{1}{4}$ cup maple syrup

2 tbsp fresh rosemary, chopped

$\frac{1}{2}$ cup Parmesan, grated

1 orange, zest only

2 tsp fresh lavender flowers

Melt the butter and combine with the olive oil and salt to taste. Pop the microwave popcorn according to box instructions. Divide the popcorn and butter-oil mixture into 3 equal portions. Add the maple syrup and rosemary to the first batch of butter, and toss it with 1 portion of the popcorn. Add the second batch of butter and Parmesan cheese to the second portion of popcorn, and toss well. Add orange zest to the remaining butter and pour it over the third batch of popcorn. Garnish with lavender flowers.

PRINCESS PARTY TIPS

1. Come up with a theme. Decide on your colors and stick with them all the way through your party.

2. Make sure there are things that people can touch and play with while at their seats.

3. When throwing a party like this outside, come up with a backup plan should the weather not cooperate.

4. Listen to what the party girl wants. The party will be a lot more fun and exciting if you plan it with her wishes in mind. It doesn't have to mean spending above your budget. It means that you might have to put on your creative genius hat, and think outside of the box.

5. Don't be afraid of getting the princess's friends involved to come up with some fun and surprises.

6. Utilize parting gifts in the tabletop decor. The less you have to clean up, the fewer things to be put in the closet, never to be looked at again.

7. Have a signature drink and give it an innovative name.

8. With a Princess Party, you are given free rein to go "over-the-top" and to make it fantastical, fun, and unexpected.

spa party

APPROPRIATE FOR:

Baby Showers

Births

Wedding Showers

Engagements

Birthdays

Spring Celebrations

Mother's Day

Easter

Wellness Events

THE CONCEPT OF a Spa Party evokes a sense

of calm, a time of renewal and replenishment

as well as a fresh, clean environment. An event that

is perfect for this theme is a shower, because a shower gathers loved ones in a tranquil and nurturing environment.

June is a very popular month for weddings, and April seems to be a very popular month for showers. The summertime also seems to be a time when mothers are planning to have their babies. Many women throughout my life have said that they prefer to NOT be pregnant during the summer months, especially during the last trimester. But then again, most of the women in my life are from places where it never gets very cold in the winter but does get very hot in the summer.

Taking all these ideas into consideration, we decided to throw a party we called "Showers and Flowers," because it combines both the freshness and nurturing aspects.

In attempting to re-create a sanctuary of calm, don't be intimidated to try to create a setting where sounds of trickling water and smells of lilies float around the room. This is one of those parties where implementing your own aesthetic and personality is paramount, while keeping it stylish and serene. It is amazing what a little "urban chill" music can do for allowing people to relax and soak in the atmosphere. Adding layers of light food and drink, as well as a variety of fresh flowers and plants to your space, goes a long way to creating the perfect atmosphere. Further, setting a table that is cheerful and colorful will hopefully make you and your guests smile, and incorporating intriguing textures and colors that coordinate with the plant and flower arrangements will tie everything together.

For this party we decided to create a template that is clean, simple, and calming. We brought in incense, candles, and flowers that created specific moods. You can probably utilize your local supermarket or a big box store to find all of the elements you will need. Imagine creating subtle undertones of citrus, mixed in with the fragrance of fresh flowers and other scents. Your space will set the mood for a very memorable time with friends and family to celebrate new beginnings. Take the time to be creative and find elements of surprise for your guests. Ask yourself how you can get the most bang for your buck. The Spa Party doesn't have to be expensive.

We decided to use the same throne chair from the Princess Party. Marley Majcher liked it so much that she wanted it at the Spa Party, as well. I personally think she just wanted to sit on it while directing everyone. Everyone had a good time with it, smiling and laughing.

When springlike weather is available, it is the perfect time for a Spa Party. Marley and I chose to design this event with a "garden" party in mind. The inspiration would come from an Asian aesthetic with clean lines and beautiful floral displays. But be prepared for the unexpected when Mother Nature is in control, and you are throwing a party outdoors. In this time of global warming, you have to be ready for anything to happen.

We originally planned to use the outdoor space, but because of unexpected rain, we decided to move the party to a patio underneath an awning that was attached to the house and just off the grassy backyard, making it an indoor-outdoor event. It was a blessing in disguise. Having to move the Spa Party under the awning made the setting unique, intimate, and protected. With the beautiful crystal chandeliers hanging over the table, we ended up creating a truly elegant surrounding! The view of the lawn was exquisite. The bamboo framed the view of the canyon and mountains beyond, creating the perfect juxtaposition of nature's creation and our own. Honestly, it doesn't get much better than that!

The Spa Party was set up for a wedding shower with thirty guests. And with most parties, things can change at the last minute, which they did, big-time. The night before, as we were hoping for the rain to stop, we were told that an additional sixteen guests would be coming. This situation definitely added unexpected stress, so Marley and I discussed all of our options. There wasn't enough room on the patio, so the late RSVPs would have to sit inside. There weren't pre-ordered place settings for these late guests, so we used Marley's own china for the additional guests and created a tabletop that would still be cohesive with the main table outdoors. Stressful? Yes! But we took a deep breath and dug in. We were either going to freak out or just do the best we could in the time frame we had, which wasn't long. In the end, it turned out beautifully. We bought extra food at the market, then we did some seating chart rearranging, and everything went off without a hitch. No one was the wiser but us.

The common thread throughout this event was wellness and health! We wanted to create a very natural spalike environment, and since the event would be during the day and outdoors, we wanted to keep it casual and fun. Our color palette was to be very cool, clean, and natural with brown and green as our primary colors. Accent colors would include white and orange and purples.

For an event like this, it is ideal to enlist someone close to you to help things run smoothly. It might be the maid of honor, the godmother, or a friend or family member, but having this extra guidance will be very helpful in what can be a surprising situation. Depending on the size of the event and your budget, you may want to consider hiring help for this event. If you are planning on having more than fifteen guests, it is smart to get as much help as you can. Don't do it alone. Also, if you and your family and friends handle the preparations, setup can be fun, even when unexpected stressful situations arise. Pour yourselves a cup of chamomile tea or a glass of champagne, and make setting up part of the event!

VISION | refreshing and clean

table and party setup

We originally planned on setting up two long rectangular tables of fifteen out on the lawn. When we moved the party under cover we had to work with the amount of space available, so we were obligated to create one long table to seat thirty.

Marley came up with an ingenious idea! She ordered several long, narrow tables and set them in two rows, side by side, connecting them but leaving about six inches in between. We then placed perpendicular bamboo poles underneath and across the two tables at the bottom corners of the support joints. Laid on top of these bamboo poles the length of the two tables were two-by-fours, so it created a sort of planter box in the middle.

We covered both rows of tables with dark chocolate brown linen tablecloths we had rented. We draped the tablecloths tightly to help create very clean lines. The cloths felt casual, yet sophisticated.

The tablecloths hung down to the floor on both sides to hide everything going on underneath the table, and because I like linens when they graze the floor. It just looks cleaner and more stylish. Ursula, who works with Marley, then created arrangements inside planter boxes, which gave the illusion of the table having a natural runner.

Once the tablecloths were placed, and the plants and flowers were in the box,

it looked like one long rectangular table, which gave the setting a communal vibe. We finished the ends of the tables with more tightly wrapped fabric to maintain our illusion and rented Chiavari chairs (with a sleek bamboo design). The fact that the chairs had an Asian vibe complemented the theme nicely. They were made of a rich soft cherrywood, which added an element of elegance that worked quite well with the chandeliers hanging above! We could have used less expensive chairs, but doing so would have taken away from the mood. In a case like this, if budget is an issue, find the money somewhere else.

environment

Even though we wouldn't be using the outdoor space as we originally planned, I wanted to be sure that the environment still looked good. Under a towering patch of giant bamboo was a beautiful sitting area composed of an oversized plastic love seat and ottoman. The rain made it impractical to use for guests, so we decided to treat it as a decorative element. We took leftover wheat grass and placed it on top of the love seat. I took the three reddish

orange tables that were stored away, and lined them up for everyone to see. This vignette was bright and fun and could be viewed from the main table. The reddish orange tables in front of the love seat tied in the details of the small orange Buddhas that would be added to the table settings.

Coincidentally, the yard had elements that really added to the environment outdoors. In back of one of the hedges, and hidden for all intents and purposes, was a beautifully shaped piece of driftwood that I thought would look great in contrast to the living vibrant green grass. So we placed it in the middle of the lawn, and it became quite literally a piece of art! This was almost karmic!

As I walked around for a final check of the space and dried the last drops of rain that remained on some of our decorative items, I realized that Marley and I had been assisted in putting this party together with the help of another very important collaborator: Mother Nature. Although the weather had been a huge challenge at the beginning of the day, it actually ended up being an influence that pushed us to be more creative.

place setting ideas

We discussed several different and creative ideas for the individual place settings. At first we even contemplated doing each place setting differently and came up with four varying options.

The first was taking a napkin and using a "butterfly" hair clip as a napkin holder and placing the napkin on the dish.

The second idea was really clever. Marley found these great wellness cards. Each card gave information on various topics, such as yoga, herbology, chakras, and more. They were inexpensive and colorful and added to our spa-like environment while still keeping it simple and fun!

The third idea was folding the napkin diagonally, and laying it diagonally across the plate. We held the napkin down with a spa brush and added an orchid to the plate to finish it off.

The fourth idea was the most simple. We folded the napkin into a square, laid it on the plate, which fit perfectly, and then put various single dried plants on top. You can take this idea and use various elements instead of the dried plant, such as crystals, rocks, or even live cut flowers and plants.

setting the table

We chose to use square white stoneware plates that mirrored the clean lines of the table. It was a nice contrast to the movement of the grasses in the floral arrangements. We set the appetizer plate on top of the main course plate. The napkins were chocolate brown linen that matched the tablecloth, adding to the organic and natural feel we were looking for. The decision to use frosted glasses added a softness that complemented both the tablecloths and napkins. Goblets were used for wine while the bucket glasses were used for other beverages. The flatware was a clean and simple stainless steel Asian design that was sleek but not obvious.

Something that Marley and I both feel is very important is the initial presentation. We made sure that everything was in line; all of the plates, every piece of silverware, every glass, and every chair were placed very precisely. This precise initial presentation leaves a lasting first impression when your guests arrive!

Although we would be serving wine and sparkling water at the main table during the meal, we also set up a bar for champagne and juices as people arrived. We used clear standard champagne flutes and the same frosted buckets that would be on the table. We created a special arrangement of flowers, plants, and other decorative items as well as the same chocolate brown linen tablecloth to tie the bar to the rest of the decor.

So our table was ready, and the bar was ready. On to the details!

DETAILS, SPECIAL FEATURES, AND GUEST GIFTS

invitations and menu design

We wanted to play off the soft, calming colors, as well as create invitation and menus that were reflective of the flowers that we would be using. Since it was a Spa Party, we thought it best to create a garden motif with a very soft organic feel, taking inspiration from a centerpiece running the entire length of the table.

The invitation and menu were made by using a base of handmade felt paper and a soft textured white paper layered over it. Keisha then hand stamped the paper with gold metallic inks and embellished them with gold glitter, grassy ribbons, and vintage buttons.

decor and gifts

Marley had several brilliant ideas that we implemented into the decor and details. Along with the flowers on the tables, we incorporated small items like brown Hindu statues and orange Buddha statues.

Refrigerated bright green gel masks were placed on several of the guests' chairs to further add to the spa environment. I tried one on for size and realized that this would be an amazing conversation piece, inspiring discussions of beauty and relaxation.

These items had multiple uses. They were part of the decor, but they were also used as parting gifts that the guests would be able to take with them. The fun thing about these party gifts is that guests can trade them, talk about them, and hopefully learn something new. Most of all, they would go home with fond memories of their experience! Along with these smaller decor items, we put together one special basket full of everything from makeup to beauty and spa products. We decided that we would raffle this gift near the end of the party as a special prize.

As a special feature we set up four spa stations. One was a makeup station. Another was for nails. The third was a chair massage station, and the fourth was a station for oxygen facials. These were certainly unexpected, making the event so much more special.

As a final parting gift, we placed small bags at the door for the guests to take as they left the party. These bags included gift certificates from the experts behind each one of the stations, as well as makeup and products that were used in each one of the stations. It was an unexpected, inexpensive, and welcome gift.

SOUND | ethereal

FOR OUR SPA Party we chose to go with a somewhat holistic spa feeling, and because of this, I chose music that was ethereal in sound. The first song, "One More Dream," written and performed by Joseph Troski, is soft and peaceful and talks about the balance one can find in another person. The words blend well with the music so as not to make it distracting.

The second song, "A Better Part of You," is a song that I wrote and recorded with my sister, Monica, on vocals and my brother, Ernesto, on Latin percussion. It is, again, an ethereal-sounding song with a down-tempo electronic beat. It has movement, but it is peaceful at the same time.

The third song, "These Burdened Years," is a little different in feel. Still soft and mellow, it is a little more pop. Performed by Joy Deyo, it is a song about a person's declaration of all of the positive things she sees in someone else despite the other person's insecurities. It's an affirming song!

TOUCH AND SMELL | dewy and green

SINCE THIS WAS a Spa Party, we wanted to evoke nature and a sense of freshness. In saying that, the floral and plant arrangements were extremely important.

The colors and textures were chosen very carefully to give our guests a feeling of wellness and health! The overall effect would be calming. We chose to go with a monochromatic and dramatic appearance. There would be a lot of "motion" and action in the flower arrangements. The stems going this way and that way, as well as the movement of the grass, would be contrasted by the stillness of small, smooth black rocks. The table was balanced and had great energy.

The most stunning arrangement was the centerpiece "runner" of the table, which was created using the "planter" that divided the table almost seamlessly. Combinations of wheat grass, ferns, and palms served as the base elements. Then tulips, lotus pods, calla lilies in white and purple, orchids, branches, rocks, and other elements added the accent colors and textures.

We wanted our guests to touch the arrangements and to be interactive with them. The flowers could easily be removed so that the hostess could invite the guests to take a flower or two as they left! And this way, not only would their senses be delighted by the floral scents during the actual party, but also hours after the event had ended. Remember, as with most of the senses, your sense of smell is deeply connected to memory. A sweet scent will be sure to conjure up lovely images and associations.

Stimulating the senses was also an important element in choosing these objects, so we placed scented sticks, packages of incense, and small bottles of aromatic oils to engage the sense of smell.

TASTE light and flavorful

To Start

baby tuscan pizzas

•

Proceed with

seafood trio of danish open-faced sandwiches

•

Followed by

charcuterie display

•

Dessert

exotic fruits and domestic cheeses

fresh pink grapefruit greyhound with candied ginger

•

*Paired with

ginger lemonade

nicolas feuillatte nv rose champagne

fresh cantaloupe martini

ABOUT THE MENU

FOR THIS PARTY, we wanted foods that were on the light side yet still satisfying and delicious. We opted for an assortment of simple yet gourmet appetizers with lots of flavor and texture. As with all of our food criteria for any event, we made sure to get only the freshest ingredients and tried to stick to organic products when possible.

baby tuscan pizzas

Little pizzas are really easy to make and are always a safe dish to prepare. It's also a great way to sneak in a vegetarian option that everyone will enjoy. Fresh tomatoes, pine nuts, roasted garlic olives, arugula—go crazy and be creative with your pizzas. Include some culturally significant ingredients or some favorite items of the guest of honor or have a "do it yourself" station, where guests can come up with their own creations and share them with the rest of the group.

seafood trio of danish open-faced sandwiches

Ronnda spent a lot of time in Europe when she was a younger chef, and she had the chance to work with butchers and fishmongers in small villages

in northern Europe. In many European countries, the butchers and fishmongers not only sell raw meat and fish but also cure, smoke, and prepare their own dishes and sandwiches for immediate consumption. Ronnda's favorites were the fresh cured salmon and fish salads they would prepare as open-faced sandwiches. These sandwiches were always the highlight of the village ladies' Saturday-afternoon tea events. Their delicate appearance makes for a beautiful display, and with only one piece of bread, it will be easy for your guests to justify having more than one.

charcuterie display

Ronnda's absolute favorite thing to prepare is a charcuterie display, and I would have to agree. Many people may get this mixed up with a deli platter with rolled slices of deli meat. When Ronnda speaks of charcuterie, she is speaking of the best dry aged hams, aged beef, and real Italian salamis available, with interesting olives, Spanish almonds, capers, anchovies, and fresh crusty breads with assorted spreads. It's a chance to try all of the new flavors available at the deli counter. First, select an upscale market by visiting their wine section. Markets that have a large wine selection with a separate department usually have all of the proper meats and cheeses to accompany them. Don't be shy about asking for samples at the deli counter. Explain that you are putting together a proper charcuterie platter complete with serrano ham and prosciutto ham and ask what other interesting things they have available to add. Don't forget to get advice on some different olive

and gherkin choices, as well as gourmet mustards and relishes that you may add to your display. Then visit the cheese counter and do the same; taste, smell, touch, and you will ultimately fall in love with the different flavors and textures. Try new cheeses like goat or raw-milk, and compare them to well-done classics like aged Cheddar and Gouda. Then throw in a wild card like Monterey Jack for fun.

nicolas feuillatte nv rose champagne

There is no better way to celebrate something special than with pink champagne. I don't drink pink champagne often, but it is very good. Widely used on Valentine's Day and around the holidays, its proper name is rose. Champagne itself is prepared from predominantly pinot noir grapes. Fresh grapes are crushed for the juice, and the grape skins are discarded. To achieve the beautiful rose color and flavor, the skins are aged for a short time with the juice, and the color is imparted into the champagne. Rose is usually a few bucks more than regular champagne, so you may want to consider a sparkling rose from California, which is usually cheaper than the French product.

THE RECIPES

baby tuscan pizzas:
mushroom, tomato-mozzarella, artichoke-olives

olive oil

12 pieces flat bread

garlic powder

salt

1 jar pasta sauce or pizza sauce (per recipe below)

fresh mozzarella, sliced

1 lb fresh mushrooms

Roma tomatoes, sliced

pitted kalamata olives, chopped fine

jar artichokes, quartered

SERVES 12.

Preheat the oven to 350°F. Brush olive oil onto the flat bread. Sprinkle with garlic powder and salt to taste. Bake the flat breads on a cookie sheet until they are slightly crisp, about 15 minutes. Remove the flat breads from the oven, and spoon pizza sauce on the flat breads.

MUSHROOM PIZZA

Top each pizza with fresh mozzarella cheese and chopped mushrooms. Bake the pizza until the cheese is melted.

TOMATO MOZZARELLA

Top each pizza with fresh mozzarella and tomato slices. Bake the pizzas until the cheese is melted.

ARTICHOKE AND OLIVE

Top each pizza with chopped olives and quartered artichokes.
Bake the pizzas until cheese is melted.

PIZZA SAUCE

    1 onion, diced
    ¼ cup olive oil
    6 cloves garlic, chopped
    2 cans plum tomatoes
    2 sprigs fresh oregano
    7 large leaves fresh basil
    1 cup red wine
    salt

In a sauce pot, fry the onions for 3 minutes with olive oil. Then
add the garlic, tomatoes, oregano, basil, and red wine. Simmer
for 30 minutes. Season with salt to taste.

seafood trio of danish open-faced sandwiches

dark pumpernickel bread

1 cup mustard

1 cup mayonnaise

4 tbsp dill, chopped

4 tbsp savory, chopped

1 head butter lettuce, cleaned

2 6- to 8-oz fresh tuna steaks

salt, to taste

1 tsp fresh cracked pepper

4 tbsp olive oil

Nova Scotia smoked salmon

½ lb cooked shrimp

Spread the bread slices onto a cookie sheet. In a bowl combine the mustard, mayonnaise, 2 tablespoons chopped dill, and 2 tablespoons chopped savory. Mix well. Spread the mixture on the bread slices. Arrange 1 piece of lettuce on each piece of bread. Separately, season the tuna with salt and pepper. Then sear in a hot pan, with 2 tablespoons of olive oil, on each side for 30 seconds (the tuna should be rare inside). Cool the tuna, slice, and arrange on several pieces of bread. Next arrange the smoked salmon over several pieces of bread. In a bowl, toss the shrimp in 2 tablespoons of olive oil and the remaining chopped dill and savory. Season with salt to taste. Arrange the herbed shrimp on remaining slices of bread.

charcuterie display

assorted cheeses, ham, etc.

exotic fruits and domestic cheeses

assorted color apples, pears, red and green grapes, oranges, tanger-
ines, strawberries, kiwi, cherries, pineapple, blackberries, raspberries,
mangoes, papaya, star fruit, bananas, and plums

chocolate-dipped strawberries

1 semisweet chocolate bar

long-stem strawberries

In a double boiler (if you do not have a double boiler, use a large pot
with a metal bowl on top), melt the chocolate until it is a creamy con-
sistency. Remove from the heat. Dip strawberries in the melted
chocolate, and cover them well. Place the strawberries on a cookie
sheet covered with wax paper. Repeat the process until all strawberries are dipped. Allow the berries to cool and then refrigerate
them until needed.

fresh cantaloupe martini

1 fresh cantaloupe, peeled and seeded

1/4 cup lemon juice

1/2 cup sugar

3 cups water

ice

Veev or premium vodka

In a food processor, combine the cantaloupe, lemon juice, sugar, and water. Blend well and strain. In a shaker add ice, 3 parts cantaloupe juice, and 1 part Veev. Shake well and pour into chilled martini glass.

ginger lemonade

1 cup fresh ginger, peeled and chopped

5 cups water

1 cup sugar

1 cup fresh lemon juice

In a pot bring the ginger and 1 cup of water to a boil. Add the sugar and simmer for 15 minutes. Allow to cool and strain. Combine the ginger syrup, lemon juice, and remaining water. Chill and serve. (This drink is perfect for kids.)

RECAP

I WAS REALLY proud of how this party turned out. It could have bombed completely, given the weather and the change in the number of guests at the last minute. But this was a lesson for me, and hopefully everyone reading this learned a thing or two as well. First, we couldn't control the weather, and given that, we made sure to have backup plans A, B, C, and D. We trusted our instincts and absolutely didn't lose our cool. We focused on the things we had to do and ultimately thought about the theme and tried to emulate that in our individual ways. Meditation and deep breathing would have probably been therapeutic, but both Marley and I thrive on this kind of pressure. Though it wasn't the most optimal situation, we brought our years of experience to the table and created an event where everyone had a great time, and no one was aware of the behind-the-scenes happenings.

SPA PARTY TIPS

1. How will the party start and how will it end?

2. Where can you get the best bang for the buck?

3. Find unexpected elements that will surprise people.

4. Have a backup plan if the weather changes.

5. Focus on the solutions not problems; pick battles when assessing your situation.

6. Always buy extra flowers since not all of them will be perfect.

Assign seating:

- Figure out where the natural break in the party is.
- Workmates and relatives won't be offended if you seat them separately.
- You don't want to seat the guest of honor apart from her friends.
- Seat the low-maintenance guests closest to the guest of honor at the main table.

white party

WHITE IS THE color of innocence, purity, and kindness, and in many cultures around the world, it represents truthfulness. I like to think of white as the beginning of something successful, a clean palette with which to work. A colorist will tell you that white is not a color like red, green, or blue. Instead, they will tell you that white is actually a combination of all colors in the color spectrum, and because of this, many people feel it is the color of perfection. Crisp and clean, white can go with almost everything. It can make a small room look larger, and a cluttered room look somehow organized and cool.

I treat white as one of the more chic colors to use in design and fashion. It's fresh, glamorous, and at once timeless, sexy, and ultimately ageless. I want your White Party to be a coveted invitation of your friends' and family's social calendars. This is about style with a cool and refreshing vibe. Now, in throwing your own White Party, I don't intend for you to throw out your furniture, rip out your carpeting, and repaint your walls. But I do want you to create a wonderland of whites, soft silvers, and very light shades of other colors that are almost but not quite white, like a very soft blush red that looks white in some light, and red in others. Incorporate these things into your space and your own design sense. I also want you to splash some color around that obviously isn't in the white family. Not a lot, mind you, but here and there. Greens or reds or oranges will create ideas with which to feed off of and become a natural bridge to your overall theme.

The next step is to go forth and accessorize, accessorize, accessorize. Set out a beautiful white leather-bound sign-in book for your guests to let you know how much they love you. Bring in white linens for the tables and chairs, white flowers for the centerpiece and accents, and white candles for lighting and visual purposes. Create white-colored drinks for some of the beverages. Of course all of these are infused with the subtle tones of other colors. One suggestion I would strongly make is to clean out any clutter that you have in the room or rooms you are going to throw the party in. I am not talking stark, cold, or impersonal. I am talking a sophisticated look that exudes elegance and style.

If you do want to take your nonwhite furniture out of the party room, and create an all-white party, you can easily rent white furniture, flokati rugs, and other accoutrements that will scream "modish glam"! I don't think it is necessary, and we won't be doing that in the following pages, but it can be a lot of fun. I have been to white-themed parties, and truth be told, these were odd and confusing. Literally, the spaces resembled cubes of white. Most of the time the only other color was a hanging glass chandelier in red or black. The couches were white, the food was white, and the cement floors were white. To me, the design was not very original and too stark. It felt like the designers were trying much too hard. I certainly can't see doing this in your home. On the other hand, should you be renting out a space, treat it as a blank canvas and create the ultimate stylish living room for your friends and family to enjoy. You can get creative, sexy, and fun. Trust your instincts, especially here. You will know what feels comfortable and what doesn't. Again, a lot depends on your guest list. How old are the people coming? Would they understand the concept? Would they feel comfortable in an environment like this, or would they stay for a bit and leave?

As for this White Party, our event planner, Tom Bercu, known for his large-scale events and fund-raisers, hosted thirty-two friends for food and drinks. We decided that this would be a party that was accessible, easy to shop for, and painless to throw together. He is of the mind that when people throw a color-themed party, it is easy to go overboard and "garbage it up," as he likes to say. No doubt a White Party in and of itself sounds daunting. When asked, most believe that a White Party has to be housed in an ultracool setting, where everyone has to dress to the nines in retro clothing or their best white designer ensembles, and where you need to have all-white furniture and spend a lot of money on all-white decorations. In reality, this couldn't be further from the truth.

VISION | white classic and luminous

TOM CONVERTED A living room into a chic dining space using bar-height square tables that sat eight people each. He decorated them with simple and stylish white accessories. The original thought was to have the tabletops sit on the floor and set back to back with comfortable white pillows for guests

to relax on. Unfortunately, once we measured Tom sitting cross-legged, we realized that there wouldn't be enough room for everyone to sit. There were a number of guests who were over six feet tall, and because of this, it would have been too confined and a bit like the game Twister, with knees and feet straddling and knocking into one another. So, thinking fast, Tom set the tables at bar height, placing white cushions on all the stools. The result was that four tables of eight fit comfortably in the space. An added benefit was that all eight people could easily talk to one another, and because many of the guests didn't know one another, it made it very easy for them to hold conversations with the entire table rather than only with their seatmates, which would have been the case had they sat on the floor. We also found that the bar-height tables, with accompanying stools, fostered casual conversations. Instead of people having to bend down to talk to someone, essentially speaking down if it was a normal-height dining chair, guests leaned in and immediately became part of the conversation in an easy, nonintrusive manner.

Additionally, a subtle undertone of Indian design was added to spice things up. Again, it wasn't something that needed to be overdone. The invitations included

a subtle Eastern flair, while the simple white silk runners with silver threading that were laid across the tables, conjured up a bit of the Indian subcontinent, as did the menu, which included curried shrimp and a roasted vegetable platter with drizzled balsamic glaze.

Again, nothing here was done in an over-the-top manner or in a way that couldn't be easily replicated. It was important for us to demystify the White Party, which over the years has been synonymous with expensive glam.

entrance foyer

I try to create design elements that will generate excitement in my guests from the moment they get to my front door. Whether it's seasonal flowers, like an autumnal wreath, or scented candles and incense welcoming one and all in a whirl of beautiful scents, I want my guests to walk in feeling the vibe that I've set for the party. If I have them commenting on the decorations even before they step inside, I am ahead of the game, not to mention it makes me feel great! Outdoor entry foyers, hallways, or paths that lead to the front entrance provide a chance to move the design from inside to outside. Most people decorate their balconies, yards, or decks, which are all great to do. However, if there is the opportunity to do something interesting and eye-catching in front of your home, then by all means, let yourself go. As soon as people get to your residence, whether an apartment, a town house, or a single-family home, they will know that something great is going on inside.

Here large storm vases lined an open breezeway that led to the front door. The overhead lights were purposely turned off to provide a more dramatic approach. This was simple to create and in keeping with the theme for the night.

Last summer I was over at a friend's house, and she was having a sushi-making party, along with sake and some cool Japanese

surface. But that would have taken away from the wood surface of the tables that we wanted to highlight and tie the outdoor deck to the interior space. We hoped that one's eye would be constantly moving back and forth from inside to out, as if it were one space. We did find fun white stainless-steel forks, knives, and spoons, but in the end we decided against them. There is no doubt that they would have fit in, but we stuck with our original purchase.

The one thing that we didn't anticipate, however, was the round-edged corners of the napkins. Corners can be tricky to fold. So we thought about fitted sheets and how you are supposed to fold those, which is obviously different from how flat sheets would be folded. With that in mind, once we got it down, we were able to fold the last napkin just before the guests started to arrive. Remember this simple tip for your next party.

DETAILS, SPECIAL FEATURES, AND GUEST GIFTS

invitation and menu design

We went back and forth over this invitation and the accompanying menu for quite some time. Did we keep the paper stark white, which everyone would expect for a White Party, or did we take into account that we were accenting this event with an Indian flavor? We opted for the latter and decided to get creative and think outside the box.

Keisha chose a clean hand-stamped henna-influenced pattern using shades of white and silvers with Indian-style silver three-dimensional embellishments and silver beading, which created a sophisticated subtlety with texture and a monochromatic palette. I think this is at once sexy and crisp-looking, keeping the White Party theme in the forefront.

heat lamps

The outdoor deck was too good a design element to pass up. We were able to make the dining area feel more spacious by accessorizing the deck with flowers, candles, and other white touches. The two spaces felt connected as one. It also allowed guests to engage one another in conversations about the view, the furnishings, or whatever else caught their eyes. Have you ever been at a get-together where people aren't talking at their tables? The party is a dud. So the more I can get people talking, the better. For the party we decided to wrap the heat lamps in white flame-retardant fabric. The whole deck took on an entirely different look. The lamps, normally ugly, stainless-steel, and utilitarian, with no design benefits, became pieces of art in their own right. It gave the deck some height, and the lamps definitely stood out among the dark green pine trees and the dark wooden planks of the deck. The fabric can be used all year, and you can change out colors to create different looks whenever you want. Bottom line, they added another layer of white in an unexpected place.

The beautifully designed green glasses with the gold leaf motif were a subtle way to add a splash of color and complement the greenery in the floral arrangements. I had no doubt that guests would take a closer look, touching them and talking about how deceptively heavy they were.

Utilizing ornate ribbon, twine, rope, and bows is a great way to add color and texture to any object. I have seen beautiful Christmas trees decorated with only colored ribbons, yarns, and decorative papers. Even though the silver ribbon was standard store-bought fare, it worked perfectly to convey the feel of an Indian-inspired party.

In trying to think of what to give the guests, while still incorporating anything purchased into the design, Tom came across these great white-chocolate lollipops on fourteen-inch sticks. Well, as you can see, we put a number of them together to make a fun bouquet of chocolate. Quirky and unexpected, they fit the party and tasted delicious!

gifts

These little leather-bound organizers were great-looking functional gifts . . . and inexpensive! I loved these because the embossed design fit perfectly with the party theme.

Since the centerpieces weren't part of the guest giveaways, we found these great little bud vases and candleholders that complemented the design, and were again functional. I know that people would place these on a cocktail table or desk. They are cute and practical gifts to give.

I wanted to include pictures of these pillows because it shows the range of pillows that you can use as accessories for any White Party. They are different shapes, sizes, and colors, but all have the common thread of being white, as well as having intricate design patterns. The green thread on one of the pillows that resembles palm fronds pulls the flower arrangements and the outdoor spaces together, while the designs on the pillow with the black thread have that henna tattoo feeling that is very Indian, in my opinion, thus continuing a common thread throughout the party. These pillows are a very easy and subtle way of reminding people as to what kind of party you are throwing.

SOUND | romantic

THE WHITE PARTY is about romantic love, so I chose songs that had romantic messages of some sort. Guy B's performance is the most vocal of this entire collection.

"Match for My Wing" is an expression of the strong belief in finding true love. We have all felt that yearning inside to find the one. Whether you are in that relationship or not, "Match for My Wing" is an eloquent way of putting those emotions into words and having faith in your match.

Guy B is an international artist born in Israel and raised in Los Angeles. His debut CD release, *Within Me,* has received rave reviews from critics. *Within Me* is a perfect blend of Pop and R&B with hip-hop and Middle Eastern influences. With groovy up-tempo songs and moving ballads, Guy B takes the listener on an emotional journey of life's many conditions.

The second song, "Crazy," performed by Renee Myara, in essence, is about a forbidden love. It is about grasping the reality that your world as you know it can be turned upside down in the blink of an eye. It explores the power of an undeniable chemistry shared by two people destined to be together. It is about the physical effects love can have on you, and how we truly cherish the romantic moments we have . . . when they are few and far between.

The third song in this collection, "Time Is Flying By," is a song I wrote and produced that has never been released before. Featuring the vocals of Rocio Mendoza, who also cowrote the song, it talks about slowing down and loving in the moment. Although romantic, this song has a loungy vibe. The electronic down-tempo composition gives this song more energy than the other two, while still keeping it in the romantic theme.

TOUCH AND SMELL | delicate and light

VIBRANT WHITE ORCHIDS, gardenias, and dahlias were beautifully arranged throughout the space that not only looked gorgeous and delicate, but smelled delicious, filling the house with light and fresh scents. Further, contemporary floral designs that included succulents and lotuses were placed outdoors, taking cues from the nature that surrounded the space.

If it were up to me, flowers would be placed in all spaces, big and small. Bottom line, flowers make most people happy. In this particular instance, since we wanted to create an atmosphere of understated elegance, we chose to highlight the flowers instead of the dishes and napkins. Ordinarily, we might have chosen patterns of dishware and flatware that were a bit more flashy with some specific design motif in mind, but creating a wonderland of light and flowers was just so overwhelmingly appealing.

Floral designer Jennifer McGarigle expressed her concern that if we went too large with the arrangements, the understated imagery would be lost. Her petite arrangements in clear glass bowls and vases played well together with the other elements on the table, neither taking away from anything else nor overwhelming the tabletop. If the arrangements were designed like they were for the Princess Party, a completely different atmosphere would have ensued, and I don't think it would have worked as well.

TASTE | spicy and robust

To Start

chilled mango soup with spiced grilled shrimp

•

Proceed with

roasted vegetable platter with drizzled balsamic glaze

•

Followed by

tandoori roasted chicken with minty marinade

and fresh basil naan

•

To Accompany

grilled chili and potato hash

•

Dessert

easy caramelized pistachio ice cream

•

*Paired with

KIDS: fresh banana milk shake

nala des reserve, spain 2005

singha indian beer

ABOUT THE MENU

BEING THAT THE theme for our White Party would have Indian influences, creating the menu with Indian cuisine was an interesting way to spice up a dinner party and seem like a true connoisseur to your friends. It seems intimidating but it is really quite simple with many premade seasoning combinations available in upscale supermarkets.

chilled mango soup with spiced grilled shrimp

Both Ronnda and I love mangoes. When you think of an exotic tropical evening, mangoes definitely come to mind. They are perfect unassuming oval curves with green and orange hues. Peel back the skin to reveal all their juicy goodness. Mangoes are comfort food. Mangoes really can make you feel good. Rich in vitamins, minerals, and antioxidants, mangoes contain an enzyme with stomach-soothing properties similar to papain found in papayas. These enzymes act as a digestive aid, and lead to a feeling of contentment.

The chilled mango soup with grilled shrimp is a perfect way to start this sexy evening. Be sure to choose ripe mangoes to get the most bang from your soup. A ripe mango should be orange and firm but give under slight pressure. Ronnda loves using them alone as a place setting or in a large vase or bowl as a stunning centerpiece.

tandoori roasted chicken with minty marinade and fresh basil naan

Indian tandoori seasoning is available from a number of spice companies. The tandoori roasted chicken can be marinated the day before to free up much-needed time on the day of your event. The extended marination time will give the seasoning a chance to creep into every corner of the chicken. One taste by your guests, and they will think you spent hours preparing this simple dish.

Naan is a traditional Indian flat bread. It is sold premade in many supermarkets. If you can't find naan, you may substitute it with any premade flat bread or pita bread (in that order). A simple basil oil will spruce up this dish and instantly become a guest favorite.

roasted vegetable platter with drizzled balsamic glaze

A roasted vegetable platter is an easy way to utilize fresh vegetables from the supermarket or your local farmers' market. These markets are great because usually you find fresh produce grown locally, instead of shipped in from another state or country. Long shipping times mean more chemicals are needed to keep the produce alive. Supporting your local farmer means fresher produce with fewer chemicals for you and your family. Many times you will find organic produce that is better for you than what may be available in your local grocery store.

grilled chili and potato hash

Grilled chilies bring a smoky flavor to any dish; it's amazing how many cultures utilize chilies in their daily cuisine. Chilies are often used in extremely hot or cold temperatures to help regulate body temperatures. Potatoes are a great canvas for grilled chilies because of their earthy flavor. Ronnda enjoys grilling with pure mesquite, but it's really convenient to use your gas grill and add wood chips to it.

easy caramelized pistachio ice cream

Ronnda enjoys using pistachios because they are found in many upscale classic gourmet cuisines. They have fallen out of vogue, she says, because of their fat content, but they're actually really delicious and make quite a splash with guests. Pairing them with a premium ice cream and dried cherries is a simple and elegantly refreshing way to end your meal. Serve this dessert at your table, or move to a more relaxed environment. It's easy for guests to grab the bowl and a spoon and lounge after such an amazing meal.

nala des reserve

Ronnda suggests the Nala des Reserve as one of her favorite wines to serve with ethnic foods. It manages to be slightly sweet, balancing strong spices while remaining intensely elegant. If you don't want to spring for the reserve, you will be quite satisfied with its little sister, the Nala NV. It's easily accessible and at around fourteen dollars a bottle, you can afford to buy more than enough to send your guests home singing. For that added bit of surprise, offer your guests the traditional Indian beer Singha. It is widely available in upscale markets, liquor stores, and ethnic shops.

THE RECIPES

chilled mango soup with spiced grilled shrimp

3 mangoes, peeled with seeds removed

4 tbsp lemon juice

1 tbsp ginger, minced

3 cups vegetable stock

cayenne pepper

salt

sugar to taste (if mangoes are not very ripe)

1 tsp garlic powder (granulated garlic)

6 large shrimp

SERVES 6.

Soak 6 wooden skewers in water for 1 hour. In a food processor, combine the mangoes, lemon juice, ginger, and vegetable stock. Blend well until it is all liquid. Remove and push the soup through a sieve or strainer. Adjust the seasoning to your liking with cayenne pepper, salt, and sugar. Separately sprinkle garlic powder, cayenne pepper, and salt to taste on the shrimp. Skewer the shrimp on presoaked sticks. Grill shrimp skewers about 5 minutes on each side or until done. Divide the soup among 6 small bowls and garnish each with a shrimp skewer.

tandoori roasted chicken
with minty marinade and fresh basil naan

1 chicken

1 tsp Kashmiri red chili powder

1 tbsp lemon juice

salt, to taste

marinade

1 cup plain yogurt

1 tsp Kashmiri red chili powder

salt, to taste

2 tbsp ground or fresh ginger

2 tbsp garlic, minced

2 tbsp lemon juice

$\frac{1}{2}$ tsp garam masala powder

1 tbsp mustard powder

fresh basil naan

1 cup olive oil

1 bunch fresh basil

1 tsp lemon juice

3 cloves garlic

salt

1 package naan or flat bread

SERVES 4 TO 6.

Wash and clean the chicken. Apply a mixture of Kashmiri red chili powder, lemon juice, and salt to the chicken and refrigerate for half an hour.

Pour whey from the yogurt and discard. Mix the Kashmiri red chili powder, salt, ginger, garlic, lemon juice, garam masala powder, and mustard powder to the yogurt. Apply this marinade to the chicken and refrigerate for 3 to 4 hours. Bake in the chicken at 375°F for 35 to 40 minutes or until the chicken is done and juices run clear.

In a blender combine the olive oil, basil, lemon juice, garlic cloves, and salt. Blend until liquid. Just before serving, brush the mixture on the naan and warm in the oven until slightly crispy. Serve immediately.

2 green bell peppers
½ onion
2 jalapeños
2 tbsp lemon juice
2 tbsp olive oil
salt
1 bunch fresh mint

Toss the green bell pepper, onion, and jalapeños with olive oil and salt. Roast at 350°F for 20 minutes. Allow to cool. Then peel, seed, and chop. In a food processor, blend the mixture with the mint into paste. Add water as needed. Salt to taste.

roasted vegetable platter
with drizzled balsamic glaze

2 red onions, cut into wedges

6 carrots, cut into sticks

2 zucchini, cut into sticks

2 red bell peppers, cut into thick strips with seeds and stems removed

2 yellow bell peppers, cut into thick strips with seeds and stems removed

olive oil

salt

3 cups balsamic vinegar

1/2 cup sugar

In a bowl toss the vegetables with olive oil and salt, being careful to keep the groups together. Place the vegetables in sections into a large roasting pan, and bake until the carrots are soft, approximately 45 minutes. Separately in a pot bring the balsamic vinegar to a boil. Add sugar and simmer until the mixture becomes a thick syrup. Arrange roasted vegetables on a platter and drizzle with balsamic glaze.

grilled chili and potato hash

3 pasilla chilies

6 russet potatoes

2 onions, cut into 6 to 8 wedges

4 tbsp olive oil

1 tbsp kosher salt

2 tbsp madras curry powder

2 sticks butter, melted

salt

pepper

SERVES 6.

In a bowl toss the whole pasillas, potatoes, and onion wedges in olive oil and sprinkle with kosher salt. Place the mixture on a baking pan, and bake for 35 minutes at 350°F or until the potatoes are tender and flaky inside. Remove the onions and pasillas in advance if necessary. Allow the potatoes and pasillas to cool. Peel the skin from pasillas and remove the stem and seeds from interior. Peel the skins from potatoes and crush the insides of the potato with your hands to get large crumbles. Dice the chilies and onions into small pieces. Toss the onions, pasillas, curry powder, and one stick of melted butter with potatoes, and season well with salt. In a baking pan, melt the other stick of butter and add salt and pepper. Place the potato mixture in the seasoned pan and bake at 400°F for 15 minutes. Serve hot.

easy caramelized pistachio ice cream

2 cups pistachio nuts

1 tsp cinnamon

1 tsp cumin

1 tsp brown sugar

1 tsp canola oil

1 quart of your favorite premium vanilla ice cream

In a bowl toss together the nuts, cinnamon, cumin, brown sugar, and canola oil. Bake the mixture for 10 minutes at 350°F. Watch them closely so that the pistachios don't burn. Remove from the oven, cool enough to handle with your hands, and remove the nuts from the pan. Scoop ice cream into bowls, and top with caramelized pistachios.

RECAP

THIS WAS DEFINITELY a fun party to put together. It wasn't as over-the-top as the Princess Party or as relaxing and chill as the Spa Party, but it was a unique way to get friends and family together for a themed party that is not usually thought of. We ate some great food, and I am happy to say that people got into the spirit. Everyone either wore something white, brought something white, or in two instances wore beautiful Indian saris in light silvers and white. When everyone was leaving, more than a handful of people pulled us aside to tell us what a good time they had had and how they now had the confidence to throw a White Party themselves, since they realized that it doesn't take a ton of work to make a space something special. It does take planning and some creativity. Trust your instincts.

WHITE PARTY TIPS

1. Start with the invitation as a hint of what is to come: the theme, the mood to be set.

2. Not everything has to be white. Focus on one or two elements, such as flowers and candles, making sure they are clearly evident in the space.

3. Utilize accessories like pillows, throws, and statuary to enhance the decor. Less is more, and if used correctly looks great.

4. Simple and chic is always better than too much stuff to make a point.

5. It is extremely important for you to not only have the theme in mind for your event prior to decorating, but to write down the mood that you want to set, keeping in mind your individual sense of style.

margarita party

Family Reunions

Cinco de Mayo

Mother's Day

Father's Day

THERE IS NOTHING better than time together with family and close friends, and the Margarita Party is perfect for intimate and fun occasions such as *Cinco de Mayo* or family reunions. For this book, I focus on family reunions, and share moments from the family fiesta that I threw for my loved ones. As you'll see from the colorful pictures and added details, this type of occasion really shows how much fun you can have with the Margarita Party theme.

With everyone working as much as they do, traffic congestion, soccer practice, doctor appointments, and travel, I fully understand how precious family time is. I know that with all the traveling I do, I cherish the time I can get my mom, my dad, my brother and sister and their kids, and all the aunts and uncles together for some good food, a lot of laughter, and some good old-fashioned gossip, of course. As my schedule has become busier, time with my family seems to be the only real time that I slow down.

While I was growing up, Mama Catita's house was the place where everyone gathered in good times and bad. It was so much fun since we are a family of cooks and we all loved to eat. Actually, we still do! I remember all the great smells that emanated from the kitchen. The *arroz* and *frijoles de la olla* were a tradition. I especially loved my grandmother's *guisados*. To this day, my taste buds get all crazy just thinking about them. I try to replicate the dish, but nothing compares to Mama Catita's *sopa de fideo*, my mother's enchiladas or my aunt's homemade flour tortillas made with lard! I remember playing games with my siblings while the cooking was going on. Either playing *La Loteria* or using our puppets, which my aunt had brought us from Mexico. I felt that I was home. I talk to my family all the time on the phone, but nothing compares to a hug and a kiss from people you love after having shared a wonderful dinner.

When we get together, especially if we haven't seen one another in a while, we like to start early in the day so there is no one rushing around or worrying about the time. Inevitably everyone has cameras, and the flashes are going off at times when one least expects, which usually makes for the best photographs.

I believe that hosting a family party shows your appreciation for the people who are most dear to you in your life. Actually that's true for any party you throw. But a family fiesta is about family, whether they are blood related or related by time and experience. I know I love it when I am invited to a party of some sort. I feel that at least someone thought enough of me to ask me over. Our family get-togethers are pretty informal. Of course there is planning involved since so many people gather at once, and we try to change the venue every so often to keep things fun for the kids and adults alike. The funny thing is that most of the planning revolves around the menu for the events. The conversations we have leading up to the events regarding food and drinks are hilarious. I always feel like I should be taping the telephone calls because everyone is making different suggestions, discussing one recipe or another, or discussing how relatives are changing their diets because they are dealing with ailments or simply because they feel that they have to lose weight. In the end, we have enough food for all of east Los Angeles, regardless of anyone's special needs. Like I wrote earlier, the get-togethers do last all day, so the food just keeps coming, which makes sense, since there is no better way to keep people gathered around one another than by serving plate after plate of their favorite dishes!

Do yourself a favor and get your family together regularly. I see my immediate family between every work trip I take, and I see my extended family at least twice a year and sometimes more. It might be hard to try to coordinate everyone's schedules, especially if there is traveling involved, but I can assure you that the memories will last a lifetime. Truly.

VISION | colorful and festive

table and party setup

For this Margarita Party, I would have special collaborators: Tom Bercu and floral designer extraordinaire Jennifer McGarigle, whose fresh and innovative work has been showcased in print and on film and TV. Together,

we turned what I know to be a traditional event into one with a modern and original twist. Charles the Chihuahua would be supervising our design as a guest collaborator and then be a guest of the party later.

The entryway was lined with clear hurricane vases with thick white candles inside of them. During the day they didn't make much of an impact, but since this was going to be an

evening fiesta, we knew that, once the candles were lit at night, the entry-way would be welcoming and exciting.

We would literally be using the entire house for this event, both inside and outside. The entryway and decking in the front of the house would be the main dining area, where we would set up a dining table. The back of the house would be set up in a more casual way. It would be very loungelike, since this was an area that resembled a cabana. The dining room inside the house would be set up as well, and the table would have many functions. At the beginning of the evening it would serve as a bar and appetizer station, and later it would be converted to an eating area for the guests.

The great thing about this house is that it had these beautiful doors that allow keeping the indoor-outdoor flow continuous. This is very important in terms of energy and also in terms of practicality for the hosts and guests. Most of the elements we would be using at this party were on the property. The items purchased were for specific and original ideas we would be implementing. The one thing we did use a lot of was flowers! Gorgeous flowers from Floral Art.

While Tom was out front setting up the dining area, Jennifer was out back getting the lounge ready. Meanwhile I was having a great time putting the gift bag together for a raffle and trying on the mini sombreros. Tom and Jennifer didn't realize that for me the fiesta had already begun!

environment

INDOORS

We used the existing dining room and dining room table inside the house as a multipurpose space. For the beginning of the party, it would serve as a place to store and display appetizers as well as a tequila bar! After all, what's a true Margarita Party without a little tequila?

The table was a bright green laminate, which influenced the kind of green elements that we would share throughout the rest of our party. Two different-sized metal vases housed trimmings of bougainvillea that we had cut from the garden. Cut-crystal candleholders and a glass tray with clear shot glasses

on it kept the look modern and clean, and our long, linear arrangement of leaves and rocks completed our beautiful multipurpose table. Also, notice the green sand that we placed between the top and the bottom of the tray. It was a subtle touch, but one that people noticed and that kept a common thread going.

We asked our guests to bring any of their favorite tequilas so that we could do a tasting and compare. I also wanted to give a small tequila-drinking lesson. You see, most people in the U.S. think that tequila is made to drink like a shot, all at once. This is far from the truth. Tequila is meant to be sipped like a fine bourbon or brandy. In fact, my favorite way to drink it is to serve it with an equal shot of sangrita, a Mexican tomato-and-orange juice chaser, and a fresh-squeezed lemon-lime chaser. Sip the tequila, sip the sangrita, and finish with the lemon-lime. *Delicioso!*

For seating here, instead of going with the metal chairs we had rented for the outdoor areas, we opted to use the eclectic grouping of different chairs already in this dining room. For the first part of the fiesta, we would have the chairs pulled away in corners and against the walls to allow for guests to have easy access to the appetizers and tequilas. Once dinner started, we would rearrange the table, set it for dining, and pull in the chairs. By keeping this cool grouping of different styles of chairs, it kept the party casual and was truly a conversation starter. Don't worry about everything matching when it comes to furniture. Some of the most beautiful rooms I have seen have had some of the furniture bought at flea markets, others at big chain stores, some at small boutiques, and still others from local artisans. It worked well because the arrangement didn't look messy or unkempt. It's like a friend curating a great installation. It tells a story, it's comfortable and approachable, but most of all, it works and looks effortless.

LOUNGE

We decided to dedicate one of the outdoor areas as a lounge. This isn't to say people wouldn't dine there later, but the setting better served casual conversation and drinks, and we knew that this was one of the places people would gather in first when they arrived.

The banquette seating was already upholstered with orange fabric, which was another defining factor in our color scheme. The pillows that accessorized the banquette and other benches at our party were purchased at a local design store. We suspended large white candles in glass fishbowls with clear fishing line, which gave the illusion that the bowls were floating in air, especially at night! It was stunning. Very ethereal and cool, and at the same time it made for a sanctuary where the guests felt comfortable.

After hanging the bowls, we began to light the candles, since some of our guests would begin arriving before the sun was down.

By the time the sun had completely gone away, we finished dressing the lounge-area coffee table with decorative elements that we had purchased for the party. Here is where you see that the base design for the party was fairly common. What ultimately gave us our fiesta feel was the decorative Mexican elements and the orange Gerber daisies that were reminiscent of Mexican daisies. By the way, the Spanish word for "daisy" is *margarita*. Appropriate, no? These small pieces really were the defining factors for our Margarita Party. With the sun down and our candles lit, the feeling of the space took a whole other turn.

OUTDOOR AND READY!

As the sun started to set, and with Charles looking over us, we began to see the light transform and our event come together. We placed green-colored sand in many of the hurricane candleholders scattered throughout the space, allowing the detail to bring together our color scheme in a way that was very creative, but simple and inexpensive at the same time.

The sand pulled from the green color of the napkins, the mums, and the glasses on the table that defined the color theme from one space to the other. The juxtaposition of the green against the browns and oranges also really helped to coordinate with the natural environment that surrounded our dining table.

From the moment our guests would reach the stairs to come into the house, they would be greeted by hurricane candleholders leading the way to the event. As soon as

they entered the house, they would be able to see the outside from the inside through the many doorways that helped to create our indoor-outdoor Margarita Party! Luckily, the weather in sunny California would be a helpful element in this style of party.

Walking through the doors and into the dining area, our guests would be enveloped by the silhouette of the palm trees in the background. The beautiful light, uplifting music, and a soothing and natural environment would immediately put everyone in a great mood. All was ready for a night of conversation, singing, dancing, and dining! It is time to celebrate life and love with family and friends. *Bienvenidos a la fiesta!*

place setting and setting the table

Jennifer had used these birds throughout the years but never painted them before. Spray painting them bright shades of orange and green was a brilliant idea that again kept the common thread, in this case color, flowing throughout the party. Orange would end up being the predominant color of the event, and the birdies would be the central concept. As an arrangement to be placed on the dining room table, Jennifer took the orange birdies and placed them in glass bowls, in which they would be supported by a nest of green-button mums sitting in a base of small white rocks. It appears as if the birds actually made their nests themselves. It was a beautiful combination of colors and elements. I'm excited about the bird theme. To me birds represent freedom and optimism. As the lyrics go to one of the songs to this event, "If you believe that birds gotta fly, they'll be clouds in the sky!"

The setup for this table would be very simple and easy to replicate. We chose inexpensive green linen napkins. We wrapped them in a single orange ribbon and then placed a little birdie on top. I'm calling it a birdie because it is so small!

The plates we used were clear glass and about the size of a traditional salad plate. This was done purposely since we didn't want the dishes to ever take attention away from the tables that they would be sitting on.

Jennifer had enough silverware, so we didn't have to go out and buy or rent more. She and Tom added whatever else they had to make sure we had enough for all of our guests, so in the end, it was a combination of many types of silverware. Eclectic and fun!

The glasses would all be blown green glass made in Mexico, so that worked really well! We used goblets for water and wine, buckets for drinks, clear glass shooters for tequila, and margarita glasses for margaritas.

DETAILS, SPECIAL FEATURES, AND GUEST GIFTS

invitation and menu design

Since this was a fiesta, we wanted to use colors that were reminiscent of the Latin culture. We went with vertical stripes and muted but passionate colors. The invitation and menu were based on having a ticket to attend. Obviously no one needed a ticket, but we wanted people to think that this fiesta was going to be a bit like a carnival, and they were special enough to gain a ticket to a very fun day.

The invitation: one ticket per person granting admission to the event using a brightly colored palette. All striping was cut from several layers of papers and placed on a solid-colored background. It was a bit like a collage with lots of cutting and pasting, but once the basic premise is down, it is easy to replicate or have copied and printed. Each place setting received a menu reiterating the idea of a festival with great food and good times.

games

When I was a child, I would play *La Loteria* with my grandmother and family. It is basically like bingo, except the dealer/announcer plays with a deck of cards that has been shuffled, and the players have cards that correspond. We played with raw, dried pinto beans as our playing pieces. This game is also a fun way to teach your guests words in Spanish. The object of the game is to see who fills his entire card first. The winner would get a wonderful fiesta gift bag!! The playing cards would also be something that the guests could take away with them as a gift.

gifts

My creative director, Steve Miller, and I went shopping to Olvera Street in Los Angeles. It's a great place to shop for a fiesta because it has preserved its pueblo feel. We bought a Frida Kahlo shopping bag made out of plastic colored netting, and filled it with wonderful gifts as well as a number of decorative items we used throughout our design.

First, I stuffed the bag with big colorful paper flowers and then filled it in with ceramic chilies on a rope, small books on how to learn Spanish, and my childhood favorite, the Mexican puppet! The how-to-learn-Spanish books can also be placed around the party for your guests to have fun with—that is, for those who don't already speak Spanish.

Other items we purchased for the bag and to spread around for decoration were mini clay mugs for sipping tequila; wooden spinning tops; a colorful ceramic box; mini sombreros,

which were also used in the lounge; and sugarheads used for Day of the Dead celebrations. In the end we spent a total of less than a hundred dollars on Olvera Street. These gifts are very inexpensive, colorful, and fun!

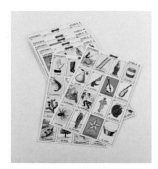

SOUND | latin

THE FOUR SONGS I chose for the Margarita Party are all definitely Latin in style. I wanted the songs to have a Spanish-flavored guitar in them to tie the three together. "*Agujita*," is the title of the first song.

Coming from a musical family, Katira has always expressed herself as an artist. As a singer she brings forth a delicious combination of introspection, musicality, and sensuality that delights the senses and stimulates the mind. "*Agujita*" is a fun and uplifting song in Spanish meaning "little needle," which is a metaphor about finding those "materials" that allow you to design your own life.

The second song is called "*A Donde Va?*" performed by Daniel Jimenez Afanador. It is a cool down-tempo dance song with a great male vocal. "*A Donde Va?*" poses a simple question: "Where Is It Going?" You sit alone in your room, and you wish to feel in love. You wish to feel confident. You wish to know where all of this is going. There is not too much to think about. "This is me at this moment. This is why I am beautiful." Afanador is a young singer, songwriter, producer from Bogotá, Colombia. His specialty is finding the essence of traditional Latin American music and bringing it to wider audiences. Most of his work is done with his band, Roxing Kafe (www.roxingkafe.com), but he gets his hands in all kinds of musical projects.

The third song in this collection is a song that my cousin gave me. Starr Kessell is a female rapper who has been working with La Verdad for several years now. They are a hip-hop group that has fused the music of their diverse cultures to create a whole new sound. Produced by Cory Yothers, "*Ya Llego*" is an edgy addition to this collection. It's a mix of hip-hop, rap, Latin, and jazz. It's a song about inspiring people to forget about their troubles and have a good time.

The last song, "Clouds in the Sky," is my first original recording in six years. I recorded it specifically for this book and for this event. It's a song I started writing many years ago, and I decided to finish it for this project. It's about living and loving life to the fullest. I took some liberties in experimenting with several styles and allowing the energy to build in the song slowly!

TOUCH AND SMELL | vibrant

THE PRIMARY COLOR for the Margarita Party would be orange, and the predominant flower would be the orange Gerber daisy. This flower would be used throughout the event in various ways.

Another flower we incorporated into this event was the green-button mum. The electric green contrasted so well against the bright shocking orange of the Gerber. I loved it! You'll notice that Jennifer used the baby mums to form these amazing nests in many of the arrangements in which the small, very lifelike birds rested in crystal bowls.

Jennifer created a centerpiece specifically for this event utilizing greenery that could be found in most gardens and the same small white rocks that would be used in the dining areas outdoors. The large leaves became this fantastic sculpture unto themselves and really made a statement. It looked fantastic and I have no doubt that you could put together something reminiscent of this look. Go into your garden, bring some of the outside in, and

create a thematically complementary centerpiece that has common threads throughout the party, such as the rocks that are being used in other areas of your party. See that. Now you are a master floral designer.

The cleverest of all of the flower ideas was the floral piñatas. Jennifer took the traditional element of the piñata and turned it into a series of floating flower arrangements. She had several hanging from various trees. Some were in the shape of spheres that were covered with orange Gerber daisies, and there were a few in the traditional Mexican shape of a star that were covered with the baby green-button mums. They added a very festive, fun, yet elegant touch to the event decor.

For most of the design, we decided to go pretty monochromatic, but we did incorporate some of the flowers from the garden like lavender-and-magenta-colored bougainvillea. These elements were both visually stimulating and great

for the aromatic influence. The lavender against a series of hurricane candles was like a beautiful natural screen. The bougainvillea was used throughout the event because we cut pieces from the plant in the garden and placed it through-out the house. Mexican fiestas are full of color, so I was happy that we added this bit of purple and pink!

table of flowers

Once again using our primary color and flower, we would use the orange Gerber daisies to create a very original idea for both the dining table and the lounge's coffee table. Jennifer had these custom bases for the tables made out of metal and plastic. The bases were a very basic design. She then had custom clear Plexiglas tops made for the table that were basically boxes with-out bottoms. They would lie on top of the table bases, and the tabletops of the bases, which were white, would became the bottoms of the clear boxes functioning as display cases.

First we cut the daisies as close to the buds as possible without damag-ing the actual flower. Then we flattened the daises as much as possible using our hands while being careful of keeping the flowers intact and not damaging the petals. One could use any flower, but flowers like daisies, which are already fairly flat, work best.

We took our cut and flattened daisies and placed them on the white table-tops in symmetrical order until the tabletops were completely covered with the flowers, hiding as much of the white tabletops as possible.

Our final step was to carefully place the Plexiglas boxes on top of the flower-covered tabletops to create our colorful table and floral display case. No doubt it cost a bit of money to create these tables since they were custom-made, but these were one of the primary elements of our fiesta.

TASTE fresh and comforting

To Start

fresh mango ceviche tostadas with avocado salsa

and

chicken wings with chipotle and chocolate

•

Proceed with

marinated skirt steak with orange and coffee

•

To Accompany

black beans with chorizo

garlic-and-cilantro rice

slow-roasted vine tomato gratiné

•

Dessert

mexican chocolate croissant bread pudding

•

*Paired with

2005 bodegas tintoralba scl higuerela grenache

KIDS: Watermelon *agua fresca*

ABOUT THE MENU

I LOVED WORKING with Ronnda in coming up with a menu for the Margarita Party. Of course I grew up with so many great foods and smells, I thought with at least this party, I could use my cultural background and come up with some great suggestions. We talked a lot about creating a contemporary twist to the traditional fiesta. I think we did my ancestors well. I have to tell you that the various dishes I sampled were out of this world. I knew we should have made more!

chicken wings with chipotle and chocolate

Why serve a little drumstick when you can serve a nice, big juicy wing? Ronnda stressed to me that it is au currant to serve gourmet wings. She calls it rustic cooking. The addition of chipotle peppers provides a spicy flavor that most people are familiar with but Ronnda includes a surprising twist of cocoa. This dish can be pretty spicy, so it's great to serve with the black beans and chorizo.

marinated skirt steak with orange and coffee

Ronnda was adamant about this dish, and I can see why. If you have not tried a traditional Mexican coffee, you are really missing out. The trick is to add a few generous shakes of cinnamon to the ground coffee before you brew. It can really spice up your morning. In the case of this lovely skirt steak, a few shakes of cinnamon go a long way. Marinate the steak in fresh-squeezed orange juice and a splash of Mexican coffee the morning of your party; then finish it on the grill just before your guests arrive. You will be astounded how easy and delicious the steak will be. The flavor was intense, and you won't taste the coffee as much as you might think. The combination of citrus and cinnamon was delicious.

tomato gratiné

This dish celebrates fresh, flavorful tomatoes in all of their splendor. One just has to look at the gloriously bright colors of these tomatoes to know that they will be sweet and full of punch. Choose an assortment of vine tomatoes for this gratiné and lead your guests in discussing the differences. There is no cutting, slicing, dicing, mashing, or anything else, for that matter. We wanted

to make this easy! Simply roasting them with fresh ingredients will really highlight their flavor. Ronnda suggested adding fresh garlic and thyme. We also included a generous amount of olive oil. Yum! When you pop the small tomatoes in your mouth or cut into the larger ones, the juices come flooding out.

black beans with chorizo

I grew up with chorizo, so eating it is second nature. But many of my friends are not at all familiar with chorizo. When they do sit down to a meal at one of my favorite Mexican restaurants, they're amazed by this flavor-packed Mexican sausage. It comes in beef or pork. The combination of chorizo, garlic, onion, and black beans is probably one of the simplest and yet most sublime flavors you will ever put in your mouth. This simple recipe can be prepared as a side dish, a main course served with fresh tortillas or a really great dip for tailgate parties. This dish always brings back great memories of sitting around the dining table with my family.

classic margarita

Served ice blended, shaken, or on the rocks, the margarita is the quintessential party drink. It's great for any type of fun event as it can be enjoyed equally for, say, relaxed beach-type themes to big family fiestas. This refreshing beverage is also the perfect accompaniment to savory appetizers. The classic margarita pairs off well with the delicious foods on the fiesta menu. And it's really easy to make. The basic ingredients are your favorite brand of tequila and some lime and lemon juice. You can also mix up the classic recipe with other different flavors of liqueur and fruit juices to make exotic and colorful variations. Just don't forget to salt the rim of your glass before pouring!

THE RECIPES

marinated skirt steak with orange and coffee

2 lbs skirt steak

2 cups orange juice

5 cloves garlic, chopped

1 cup brewed coffee with cinnamon

1 onion, chopped

1/4 bunch cilantro, chopped

salt

pepper

1 dozen corn tortillas

Salt and pepper skirt steak to taste. Separately combine the orange juice, garlic, and coffee in a bowl, and mix well. Pour the orange juice marinade over the steaks, and add the chopped onion, cilantro, salt, and pepper. Cover and refrigerate for at least 1 hour (you can marinate steak for up to 24 hours). Heat your grill to 400°F.

Remove the tortillas from the package, wrap them in heavy-duty foil paper, and place on the grill.

Place the skirt steak on the hot grill for approximately 5 to 8 minutes on each side (vary according to thickness of meat). The meat should be slightly pink inside when done. Allow the meat to cool slightly, slice it into thin strips, and serve it with the warm tortillas.

fresh mango ceviche tostadas with avocado salsa

½ lb small or medium-size raw shrimp, peeled and deveined

½ lb bay scallops

2 cups fresh lemon juice

1 tsp lime zest

1 tsp cumin

salt

pepper

1 red bell pepper, diced small

½ bunch cilantro, chopped

3 green onions, chopped

1 jalapeño pepper, diced small

1 dozen corn tostada shells

Avocado Salsa

3 avocadoes, peeled and seeds removed

2 tbsp lemon juice

2 Roma tomatoes, diced small

½ onion, diced small

salt

pepper

Rinse the shrimp and scallops well and place in a pot (preferably glass). Add the lemon juice, lime zest, cumin, salt, and pepper. Bring the shrimp and scallops to a simmer. Turn off the fire and allow the seafood to cool. Put the mixture in a glass bowl, and add the bell peppers, cilantro, onion, and jalapeños. Refrigerate a minimum of 4 hours.

Chop the avocadoes into small cubes. Put them in a bowl, and add the lemon juice, tomatoes, onion, salt, and pepper. Cover and refrigerate until ready to serve.

Just before serving, place 3 large tablespoons of ceviche on a tostada shell, and top with 1 tablespoon avocado salsa.

chicken wings with chipotle and chocolate

1 can chipotle peppers in adobo sauce

2 lbs chicken wings

garlic powder

chili powder

salt

pepper

cocoa powder

Strain the chipotle chilies, and reserve adobo sauce. Toss the chicken wings with the garlic powder, chili powder, salt, and pepper. Pour the adobo sauce over wings and toss well. Bake the wings at 350°F for 30 minutes or until done. Remove the wings from the oven, and sprinkle them with cocoa powder. Serve with the chipotle peppers on the side.

black beans with chorizo

1 lb black beans
1 onion, diced in large chunks
10 cloves garlic, smashed
1/2 lb chorizo sausage
2 qts chicken stock
salt, to taste
pepper, to taste

Soak the black beans overnight in warm water. Place the black beans, onions, garlic, and chorizo sausage in a pot, and add the chicken stock. Boil about 1 hour or until the beans are tender. Add water if needed. Season with salt and pepper to taste. Serve warm.

garlic-and-cilantro rice

2 cups long-grain rice
4 cups water
2 tbsp olive oil
5 cloves garlic, chopped
1/4 bunch of cilantro, chopped
1/2 tsp salt

Combine all the ingredients in a glass baking dish, cover, and bake at 350°F until all the water is evaporated and the rice is tender, approximately 20 minutes.

slow-roasted vine tomato gratiné

4 to 6 red tomatoes on the vine

6 to 8 red cherry tomatoes on the vine

4 to 6 yellow tomatoes on the vine

6 cloves garlic

4 sprigs thyme

olive oil

salt

pepper

SERVES 6.

Place all the tomatoes with stems and garlic in a glass baking dish.
Cover them with the thyme, olive oil, salt, and pepper. Roast about
35 to 45 minutes at 400°F or until well roasted and the tomato skins
split. Then put the tomatoes under broiler for 1 minute. Serve warm.

mexican chocolate croissant bread pudding

2 cups heavy cream

2 cups Mexican chocolate, chopped into chards

1 cup sugar

2 egg yolks

6 day-old croissants, cut into cubes

1/4 cup raisins

1 stick butter, melted

In a sauce pot, bring the heavy cream to a simmer. Turn the fire down; add the chocolate chards and whisk well. Add the sugar and egg yolks, and whisk well. Turn off the fire. Put the croissant cubes in a bowl and cover them with the chocolate mixture. Add the raisins and melted butter. Cover the mixture and set aside for at least 1 hour. Coat a baking dish with nonstick spray, and bake the bread pudding at 350°F for 25 minutes or until slightly crusty on top.

the classic margarita

3 parts premium tequila
1 part fresh squeezed lemon juice
1 part fresh squeezed lime juice
1/2 part premium clear orange liqueur
2 tbsp Rose's lime juice
1/2 cup of raw sugar
lime slices
1 tsp salt, and additional salt for rims of glasses

In a large pitcher mix all ingredients except lime slices.

Salt the rim of your glass and garnish with a slice of lime!

For "on the rocks," pour the mixture into an ice-filled glass.

For "ice blended or frozen," put about 1 cup of ice and mixture into a blender on medium speed for 5 to 10 seconds. Pour into a glass.

For "shaken," fill a shaker with ice, add the mixture, and shake well. Pour into a glass.

watermelon *agua fresca*

1 whole watermelon, peeled and cut into large chunks
2 cups water

In a food processor, blend the watermelon and water. Strain, chill, and serve. (This drink is perfect for kids).

THE BLUE MARGARITA

Same as the classic margarita, but substitute orange liqueur with blue curaçao and garnish with a lemon.

THE MINT MARGARITA

Same as the classic margarita, but substitute Rose's lime juice with mint liqueur. Garnish with fresh mint!

THE POMEGRANATE MARGARITA

Same as the classic margarita, but substitute lemon juice with pomegranate juice.

JAMAICA MARGARITA WITH CUMIN SALT

> 1 cup *Jamaica* leaves
> 4 cups of water
> 2 cups sugar
> ice
> margarita mix
> premium tequila
> lime wedges

In a pot bring the *Jamaica* leaves and water to a boil. Add the sugar and strain. Fill a shaker with ice; add ¼ cup *Jamaica* syrup, 1 cup margarita mix, and ¼ cup tequila. Shake well and pour into a glass. Garnish with a lime wedge.

RECAP

A FAMILY FIESTA can be very inexpensive and easy to create. Because it has a Latin flair, any, and many, colors can be used. It is easy to mix and match things around the house, and don't be afraid to be too bold! This is a great event to bring your family together, or those friends who are closest to you, and because it is so easy, you can invite as many friends as you want. A fiesta is very informal and should always be fun. It's about getting together, eating, singing, and dancing, so go get your sombrero and enjoy! To me, all of life should be a fiesta. Fiestas are synonymous with celebrations and happiness, and I am proud to come from a culture that celebrates it so well. In my Latin culture, celebrating life is just as important as working hard. There is no point in working hard and making a lot of money if you do not have the time to enjoy it and the opportunities to share it with the ones you love. *Salud!*

MARGARITA PARTY TIPS

1. You can use ANY color scheme for your Margarita Party.

2. Mix and match colors and design elements, and use anything you already have in your space.

3. In order to invite as many guests as you like, use both the inside and outside of your home.

4. Shop at a local Latin store or *bodega* to find fun, colorful, yet inexpensive elements.

5. Be sure to make all of the music lively! Dancing is encouraged at a fiesta!

6. Include elements that encourage learning or speaking Spanish. Your guests will love it!

7. Have at least one dish that ties into your culturally themed fiesta. Not everything, mind you, has to be thematically the same.

8. Make sure that there is some fun food to eat that both adults and kids can talk about, use their hands with, and even tell funny stories about. Adults might remember something from when they were growing up that involved a certain dish. If your family is in attendance, it is a perfect opportunity to add a dish that might be an inside joke for your immediate family. All in good fun.

summer party

A LONG WEEKEND during the summer, when everyone is off from either school or work, is the perfect time to throw a party. And where better during these lazy, fun, indulgent weekends than at the beach or your local park. Both are fun and relaxed, and they generally come with built-in activities. The easiest informal get-together is throwing a picnic. What could be better than to have the sun shining and warming your skin? If you are at the shore, the waves crashing against the rocks or cresting on the sand create the perfect sound track. There is something about both these places that makes a get-together so special. People "switch off" and relax. I strongly believe that the visual and audio cues, whether at a state park, at a mountain retreat, or on a sandy stretch of beach, are ones that allow people to let their minds wander and to reset their internal clocks. I don't care if you are a type-A accountant, lawyer, or stock-broker. A few minutes in the right environment will bring down your blood pressure and make you a healthier person.

I chose to include an event that could easily be adapted to the beach or the park, simply because these are fun places to gather, and most people don't take advantage of nature's wonders. Whether you are in a big city or a small town, there will be havens of green space in which to picnic. Should you be lucky enough to reside in an area close to a public lake or along the coast, then you have no excuse whatsoever not to gather your belongings and head down to the water's edge. Also, over the years, water elements have become increasingly important in all of my design work. I have found the sounds of nature to have a very grounding effect on residential spaces.

For this specific party, we chose a beach location. As you will see, it is more formal than just throwing a blanket down on the beach and setting out your plates. However, this environment doesn't have to be any more daunting than anywhere else. We have basically transferred the event to the outdoors. I wanted to do this in order to show how simple it is to create different atmospheres using the same thoughtful planning.

For a more casual gathering, here are some thoughts and tips to keep in mind to make your day and weekend a wonderful one. Get creative and come up with a theme you love and carry it throughout the event . . . from the food to the decor and guest giveaways. Have your guests dress accordingly. The fun factor will go way up, and the mood will most definitely be enhanced. To lay out your party, find a place that is not too windy. There are not many things worse than having your blankets, plates, and cups blowing all over the place and making a mess before you even start. As with any sit-down event, plan your menu based on the number of guests invited. Also, remember that you can only carry so much, so base it on ease of transport, as well. You can also request that your guests bring their own chairs and blankets or towels to lighten your load. In addition to the food and beverages, don't forget an umbrella and a hat to keep from getting sunburned. Also pack an umbrella for the food, to keep the sun from making things go bad. Freeze water in plastic bottles instead of bringing ice. For the most part, these will keep things colder for longer. Once the ice melts, you will have extra water to use as drinks. Check with local government offices to find out about the laws regarding trash pickup, glass, alcohol, and fires, whether they be barbecue or bonfire related.

For this picnic on the beach, we had twenty-four people join us. We chose colors that were reflective of our environment: yellows and blues as well as soft pastoral colors that were reminiscent of the outdoors or a field of wildflowers. We also chose linen that would not ordinarily be a first choice for most people. It was dark and somewhat forbidding, but at the same time, it was a spectacular fit with the sand and surf. We needed to make sure that the colors complemented one another, the floral displays, and the venue where we chose to have our picnic. We made an effort to keep this relaxed and very "unnautical." Otherwise it would have been expected and too easy, and as you know, we LOVE the unexpected. The unexpected also led us to create a candy bar using the beautiful Waterford crystal as displays to house some delicious sweets. Now that was fun and filling!

We had a good time setting up a beach blanket made out of burlap. Sure, we could have used a sheet or a beach towel, but this was different and *unexpected*. We thought that some of the adults and kids might want to stretch out on the sand and take in the surroundings. We set the blanket the same way as the tables, for the most part. However, in addition to the cups, plates, and napkins, we laid out a treasure chest with pashminas and shawls, in case it got cold as the sun went down. More on these elements later in the chapter. So, without further ado . . .

VISION | relaxed and breezy

table and party setup

We wanted to make this event as easy as possible, not only for us, but for all of you when it is time to plan your sit-down picnic. By that, I mean, why make difficult what should be a drama-free party, right? So we decided that three round tables of eight would work out well. They wouldn't take up large amounts of space, each being around sixty inches in diameter, while the chairs were standard size. We happened to have one of the tables already, so we only had to rent the two additional tables and the chairs. Since a tablecloth covered the entire table, without the legs showing, the condition of the tables or the fact that the tables wouldn't match didn't matter. Round tables foster conversation, and seating for eight allows everyone to interact and talk with one another freely. Larger tables or a different configuration would have made the atmosphere a bit more formal, in my thinking, and not as carefree as it ended up being.

The tables were situated with a view of the ocean, of course, but also in an area of the beach where the people sitting with their backs to the

Pacific would be able to look at a lot of sand rather than at a parking lot. Mind you, we couldn't get too close to the water because with the weather so great, there were large amounts of people on the beach, so we chose an area where we could have some room to ourselves but also be close enough to the water should the guests want to walk down to the water's edge and put their toes in the really, really cold water. It might have been balmy on the beach, but that water was arctic!!! What this all means is that you need to know your venue. We are at the beach, so of course you want to see the ocean. If you were at a park, you might want to situate yourself under a majestic tree or in view of a monument in the park. If you have neither, you might want to create your own visual landscape with the accessories you use.

We rented the white plastic chairs because they were inexpensive, right for the windy and sandy conditions, and I loved the way they stood out against the dark charcoal.

They weren't in the best condition, but since this was an informal affair, we thought that it wouldn't matter so much. I know we have written in other chapters about complementary colors and common threads, and these chairs do work well with the light and airy qualities of the flower arrangement, but they also look great aesthetically.

Notice that the tablecloth hangs to the ground and actually puddles. Ordinarily, I don't like puddling linens. I like linens that "kiss" the ground, creating very neat and linear lines, but again, because this event was a picnic at the beach, I wouldn't be so strict with myself. Truth be told, Marley and I went back and forth a couple of times, but each time the linen hit the sand, it just looked so cool. I would have been outvoted, anyway, since everyone else helping with the setup loved the way it looked. The crinkled-and-crushed texture of the linen was an added plus. It shimmered in the sunlight, changing back and forth from a deep charcoal to a cool dark purple. The material looked like a very heavy piece of material, almost like drapery fabric, the kind that could block out the sun even at its brightest, but it was superlightweight and easy to deal with. It would make no sense to bring something so heavy to the beach. First of all, it had to be carried to the location. Second, if it got wet or dirty, cleaning it would

be difficult, to say the least. In fact, the silk was almost sheer. It was so deceptive that we chose to use the same fabric for the napkins. We decided to use larger napkins and fold them over a few times so that they were thick enough. Because they looked so gutsy, they seemed much more luxurious than they actually were. The charcoal-on-charcoal effect was interesting and allowed the plates and glassware to stand out from the table.

We did take some liberties because we wanted to do some things that you normally wouldn't see at a picnic, especially not one at the beach. Thanks to our friends at Waterford Wedgwood USA, a candy bar consisting of Waterford crystal filled with all sorts of candy including saltwater toffees supported our beach theme. Visually beautiful handmade lollipops, as well as an assortment of treats that you would remember well from your childhood, would be totally unexpected.

The goodies were showcased in fourteen Waterford crystal urns, vases, and platters. The crystal was placed on two eight-foot rectangular tables that were standard banquet size. These were rented as well and also quite inexpensive. We covered the tables with simple white tablecloths, which played off the chairs close by and didn't take away from the main attraction, the candy. We had old-fashioned scoopers with ribbons that reflected the assorted colors on display, carrying through the common threads and complementary elements of the event.

The scoopers alone allowed for a very romantic touch and brought me back to the days when I used to go to a small candy store with jars filled with candy that were displayed so nicely on old worn shelves. When I think back, I remember that the floors of the candy store were badly scuffed and worn, but that was part of the allure. The smell was a mixture of candy and wonderful woods that were probably around for decades before I started going there. Like many places that I have fond memories of, the store is gone, but I remember how comfortable I felt in that space. I am sure that the owners had a lot to do with it, but at the time, I could only focus on the caramel-glazed apples and the chocolate-covered pretzels I was about to sink my teeth into.

The Waterford crystal was of different shapes and sizes. Some were of the cut-crystal variety and some were not. Both Marley and I love to play around with the height of various elements in a design scheme. How the candy was displayed was as important to us as the candy itself. Most times, candy comes in cardboard boxes or plastic bags, and it is up to you to figure out how to lay it all out. We wanted a big presentation showcasing the candy to make it look big and abundant, as well as interesting. Footed and wider containers, versus narrow ones, often make whatever you are showing off appear bigger and better. If you don't have a suitable piece, place the containers on risers or on books to make them look higher. Then place complementary fabric on top

of the risers so as to hide them. It's literally about first split-second impressions that guests make.

We wanted to treat the candy table as a buffet, where people could get up and take as much or as little as they wanted. We also placed see-through plastic boxes that look like Chinese-food takeout containers. At the end of the evening, everyone could take home doggie bags or, in this case, boxes full of their favorite candy, which meant a lot less to clean up and a lot less candy for me to be able to eat at home.

Of course you don't have to use Waterford crystal to make a great confectioner's table. Clear plastic tubs filled with candy or any other interesting container would have done the trick. Just make sure the neck is large enough for the scooper to fit into. Also, should the candy container not be of any design significance, put something around it like ribbons or pictures of the guests attending, or name each container after one of the guests. It will surely get people laughing and talking among themselves. Just make sure that you don't make someone feel bad by putting his name on a container. It should be in good fun, but if someone is body conscious, it is best to avoid naming a tub of candy after him.

There are so many things that could be used to hold the candy. Polypropylene and cellophane plastic bags are found everywhere from florists to candy stores. They are essentially clear little bags. They are often called corsage bags and come in a multitude of colors and patterns. You can find the Chinese-style takeout containers at your local Chinese restaurant, or should you like that shape but want something fancier, card and gift stores are selling great high-gloss takeout containers that will definitely add color to your table. I like the clear ones myself, since they show off what is inside. Go out and buy some stickers that relate to the party, and use them to seal the bags or to stick on the takeaway boxes in a fun manner. If you are throwing a smaller party and have some money to spare, find a higher-end container that you can give the guests as a party favor they can use for other purposes in their homes.

a few tips regarding any candy buffet

Think of your candy buffet as you would a cheese buffet or platter. Any good cheese presentation would include an aged cheese, a blue cheese (color), a soft cheese, a hard cheese, and a fragrant cheese.

Balance the candies. You don't want all chocolate and nothing else. Marley thought of an apt metaphor. If you are throwing a dinner party, and you know that one of the guests only eats vegetarian, you shouldn't have to tailor the whole menu around this person. Of course you come up with dishes that he or she will love, but add other foods that your five, six, or ten other guests will enjoy as well. So, with candy, have some chocolate, some sweet candies, some sour candies, and candy with textured insides, like caramel or crème or fruit centers.

It is also fun to tailor the color scheme of your candies. It is not as hard as you may think. For example, if you think of sherbet colors, you immediately think of washed, soft rainbow colors, but without the reds or blacks.

Also think about the size of your candy. Have long rope candy, short, fat candy, individually wrapped candy, and others like M&Ms and Red Hots. You should buy things that will stick out and not be just another element. I want your candy to have some personality. If you are going to highlight, say, an awesome French gourmet hand-dipped chocolate with all sorts of amazing tastes, then I would suggest toning down the rest of the offerings and displaying licorice, toffee, and candy buttons. This leads me right into the fact that generic bulk candies are a great filler. You get more bang for the buck, and you can really fill up the container you use to make it look like a massive offering.

We started to notice that some of the candy was sticking together and some was melting. So don't do as we did and lay out the candy hours before the event is to start. If you do, at the very least place a light-colored linen over each one to deflect the sun. If you have a large umbrella for shading purposes, that's even better. I am told that you could put some ice wrapped in a bag and place it under the candy to keep it cool. But if you do this, for the sake of the

beach blanket bingo

I know what you're thinking: Why burlap? And I say
to you, why not? It was with the same mind-set that
we set out pink candles at the Princess Party during
the day. Anyone can put out a beach towel, blanket,
or bedsheet. But if there is one thing that I have been
stressing over and over, it is for everyone to step out
of the comfort zone. Burlap makes me think of that
I Love Lucy episode when Lucy and the gang go to
Paris, and Ricky and Fred make burlap dresses for
Lucy and Ethel, then tell them that they were one-of-
a-kind haute-couture evening wear. Anyway, while
burlap isn't a coveted fabric, it did make for a perfect
beach accessory. I didn't worry about getting it dirty.
Burlap is a sturdy material able to withstand a lot of
wear and tear, and it is unexpected! Kids can run all
over it, and it won't rip. You could keep it for a long
time if you wanted to. We actually frayed the edges
to keep it loose and relaxed. It isn't hard to do at all.
Just take a loose thread on the horizontal and pull. We
wanted this blanket to have some personality. It was
a very conscious decision.

We decided it would be first come, first seated on
the blanket. But you could just as easily have all the
kids sit on the sand or have the parents and their children sit together on the
blanket. Inevitably, everyone is drawn to the blanket anyway, since it is such
a conversation piece. If you like the idea of the beach blanket for formal dining you could run two long swatches of the fabric facing each other along the
beach and sit family-style. The bolts of cloth are usually quite wide, so dining on them wouldn't be a problem. We also thought to raise the beach blanket a few inches by utilizing milk crates and two-by-fours; so while you sit on

the beach and sand, your food doesn't. In the end we wanted a true beach blanket experience, and that's what we got.

We set the beach blanket for four people with the same place settings as on the sit-down tables, except we placed white napkins to make it a little less formal. It tied together nicely. You could very easily add some color and pizzazz to the white napkin by adding some elements from the candy buffet as well. The tray at the center of the blanket can serve many different functions. By the way, you can find trays like this almost anywhere these days. You could easily stack the dishes on the tray along with everything common to the rest of the table, like the silverware and glassware, and not worry about them falling over. The tray can also be used to stabilize your floral centerpiece without having to dig a hole to make sure it doesn't go flying should someone walk by.

You'll also notice that we used the tray to place a paint can full of gifts. The can is cheap and functional. We placed in it all the giveaways, like sunscreen, lip balm, handy wipes, paintbrushes, and baby powder. The paintbrushes were to wipe the sand off, while the baby powder allowed our guests to easily get rid of the sand that was sticking due to perspiration. I love the paintbrush idea. How many times are you at the beach and you get sand all over your car? Well with a cheap paintbrush, it is easy to wipe the grit away. The kids can also use the can to make sand castles and the like. We wanted everything to be functional and fun. It would be very easy to come up with two sets of cans, one for kids and one for adults. The adult container can have disposable cameras, miniature chess and checker sets, tarot cards, small shot glasses, and mini bottles of alcohol. If it was a special occasion, you can customize everything so that your giveaways and accessories are branded with names and dates. It is fun and definitely memorable.

The milk crate that I mentioned earlier had clothing, flip-flops, and other articles of clothing that people might want to borrow should they get cold. It was a fun touch and one that made people think they were going into someone's closet. It also had the feel of a treasure hunt—well, maybe "scavenger hunt" is a better term in this case. Whatever the correct term may be, the milk crate was fun and served as another great conversation point.

People were definitely enjoying it because it made perfect sense to have it there, although no one ever actually does it.

We placed tiki torches around the blanket to give it a balmy, island feel. You could just as easily put out citronella candles that serve to keep the bugs away. One thing that we didn't do, and I wish we had, was use surfboards. We were thinking of utilizing the board as part of the buffet, but in the end we thought that it was a bit too over-the-top, even for us. But it is a fun idea. And if you can work it into your design scheme, go for it.

I have to tell you that this was a lot of fun, and the friends and family who came out were inspired by all of the creativity that we displayed. Use a little forethought, and you will most definitely have a picnic that your guests will not soon forget. It would be so easy to have this in your backyard, the local park, a communal area of your apartment building, or any pretty location you can think of. Think colors, interesting displays, great food, and of course, nice people.

SOUND | funky and uplifting

"OK ALRIGHT," PERFORMED by a group I was just introduced to called Helios Jive, is funky, fun, and uplifting. The Summer Party is all about having a good time with family and friends outdoors on a beautiful day. This song is very original and I chose it for the message, "I'm OK. I'm alright. . . ."

The second of the two songs I chose for this party is a song I wrote, recorded and released on a collection while I was signed with Mythic Music Group in San Francisco. "Everybody Stand Up" (XoLeo Mix) was coproduced with Leo Frappier. For this song we chose to blend electronic Latin and jazz together. It's a song about getting together with family and friends, putting your hands in the air, and dancing!! No worries, just fun!

TOUCH AND SMELL | airy and aromatic

WE DECIDED ON simple floral arrangements for our picnic. This party is all about the surroundings. While a gorgeous floral display can upstage almost anything, having miles of beautiful sand and ocean surrounding us allowed us to concentrate on flowers that gave off great scents. When we were placing the flowers on the table, it was as if we had sprayed the table with liquid flowers. This is not always a good thing, mind you. If we were inside, it would have overpowered the food and taken away from the experience, but we were outside, and with the breeze, it was perfect. Think about a woman with a lightly scented floral perfume versus being stuck in an elevator with a guy who put on one too many handfuls of cologne. It is one of those "aha" moments!

The flowers reminded me that this event was truly about the senses. We have the water, the sounds of life all around, some great food, the flowers, and this very cool fabric that I can't stop playing with. It isn't just me. Everyone else is crinkling the fabric as well! My intuition told me that this was the right spot to hold a picnic. I trusted myself, and the results were amazing. I

think naming the candies after aunts, uncles, and best friends was the biggest hit. So, with the flowers, Marley thought that a light, airy display full of aromatic flowers was the way to go. But it wasn't a thinly put-together arrangement. This arrangement was all about abundance! Cymbidiums, roses, dahlias, peonies, and hydrangeas sprang forth like a leopard hunting its prey. I like her way of thinking. Give your guests more than they expect. Show them that abundance is a great thing. All three tables had the exact same flowers because they were each so aromatic. Unlike the Princess Party or the Spa Party, where the design was tightly controlled, the fact that we were outside on the beach made everything have to be looser and more relaxed. It was a conscious decision and a conscious effort to do this. You have to know your venue.

A "scentscape," much like a "tablescape," creates imagery for all the picnic attendees. No doubt some of the people around the table thought of botanical gardens. Others might have thought of their family gardens when they were younger, while others might have thought of the great flower expo they had gone to the week before. Regardless of the memory, it would no doubt be a good one, and that's what we cared about. I would say that out of the twenty-four people, a good twenty of them bent down to smell the flowers. It was good to see.

Being that the flowers were in the hot sun for a few hours, we had to make sure that there was plenty of water at the bottom of the arrangements. The flowers were beautiful, and although we didn't have to, we also spritzed the blooms with water at various intervals to try to keep them looking fresh and perky. I don't like to see droopy vines on my tables. At the end of the evening, the three centerpieces were given away to the individuals who guessed closest as to how many caramel candies were in one of the dishes. Of course, we had to keep track of how many my coauthor Steve Miller ate while setting up and subtract from there. It was a fun raffle and people love games. It was very funny watching the kids and some adults putting their noses right up to the glass to see how deep the base of the crystal dish went. People are competitive, and they wanted a centerpiece!

TASTE | rich and smoky

To Start

fresh tomato salad with olives and orange

•

Proceed with

juniper-crusted smoky lamb leg (leg, chops, or loin)

or

maple smoked whole salmon with fresh herbs

•

To Accompany

grilled corn with chili butter

fire-roasted yams with whipped butter

•

Dessert

slow-grilled pineapple with key lime crème fraîche

•

*Paired with

KIDS: mint lemonade

basil white wine sangria

ortman pinot noir, central coast california

ABOUT THE MENU

RONNDA AND I talked a lot about what people would want to eat when they know they have a long weekend ahead of them, or possibly want to do something different from the standard picnic. Well, ladies and gents, we give you different. If you take anything away from this book, it is the fact that you can create wonderful and sensual events by thinking out of the box a little bit and testing the creative waters. You can do it. You just have to trust yourself!

juniper-crusted smoky lamb leg (leg, chops, or loin)

If you can find juniper berries, Ronnda told me, you are in for a treat. She says that they are no doubt the most exciting seasoning that no one uses. And you know that I love finding new things and running with them. And now I get to introduce it to you. No doubt many of you cook with juniper berries already, but for those of you who don't, you are in for a treat. I learned that they can really enhance game-flavored meats like lamb, venison, and buffalo. If you combine the juniper berries with hickory smoke, you have pure magic, as Ronnda likes

to say. Make sure you start with a mild-flavored lamb leg. Ask your butcher for flavor profiles of the lamb you are purchasing. People who claim they don't like lamb usually are turned off by an intense game flavor. Choosing a mild-flavored lamb will make your dish more appealing to a multitude of palates.

maple smoked whole salmon with fresh herbs

You should follow the same rules when purchasing salmon as you do lamb. While wild salmon has more healthful attributes, its flavor is very strong. When cooking for a large group, choose a farm-raised salmon for its more mild flavor. You will also save yourself lots of money. The price difference in wild salmon and farm-raised salmon can be as much as eight dollars per pound. If you have a small group, just purchase one side of salmon instead of a whole one.

grilled corn with chili butter

A picnic is not a picnic without grilled corn. Only here we decided to spice things up and add some chili butter. Yes, it is a little spicy, but you can season the corn to your liking. Besides, how often do you get some zing with your corn? It was actually a lot of fun to make this dish. Not only was it quick and easy, but I felt like a chef. And best of all, it was delicious.

minty lemonade

Over the course of several days, I learned a lot about Ronnda and her background as a chef. She has worked hard to get where she is! One of the stories involved the first bar mitzvah she had catered as a favor to an old college friend. She laughed when she told me that one of the many things that stood out about that day, was the first request she ever received for minty lemonade, but she has had the same request at every subsequent bar and bat mitzvah. She said the kids absolutely love it, while the adults love to mix it with vodka. Sounded good to me! What made this lemonade so irresistible? The secret ingredient, she whispered, is maple syrup. It seems that maple syrup blends perfectly with the mint and adds a slightly nutty flavor to the lemonade. This recipe is perfect to share with family and friends for any holiday grill or barbecue party.

ortman pinot noir

One of my favorite parts of coming up with the menus is the wine pairings. We have to choose which wine tastes best with what. Of course, I didn't want to let anyone down! Ronnda's first, second, and third choices for this menu were the Ortman Pinot Noir. We tried a few other wines, but I, too, kept coming back to this wine. While most people may choose a cabernet with steak, this particular pinot noir is very full-bodied and not very tannic. Ortman is a small family-run winery on the central coast of California. The father has long been a winemaker, and he brought his son into the business. It was a perfect marriage of old-school techniques and new-school technology. They have succeeded in making a family of delicious food-friendly wine with extraordinary character.

THE RECIPES

juniper-crusted smoky lamb leg
(leg, chops, or loin)

2 cups hickory chips

2 cups red wine

3 tbsp juniper berries, crushed

4 tbsp fresh thyme leaves

4 tbsp fresh rosemary leaves, chopped

10 cloves garlic, chopped

¼ cup olive oil

sea salt or kosher salt

fresh pepper

1 leg of lamb

3 carrots, chopped into large chunks

2 onions, chopped into large chunks

1 stalk celery, chopped into large chunks

SERVES 6 TO 8.

Soak the hickory chips in red wine for 1 hour. In a bowl, combine the juniper berries, thyme leaves, rosemary, garlic, olive oil, salt, and pepper. Place the soaked wood chips on a hot grill, and wait for the chips to begin to smoke. Spread the herb mixture generously onto the lamb, and place the lamb on the grill for 30 minutes. In a roasting pan, place the carrots, onions, and celery. Remove the lamb from the grill and place it on top of the vegetables. Bake in the oven at 350°F for approximately 1 hour, or until the thermometer reads 135°F (medium-rare).

maple smoked whole salmon with fresh herbs

2 cups wood chips

2 cups white wine

1 whole salmon or side of salmon

1 cup olive oil

2 tbsp fresh rosemary

4 cloves garlic, chopped fine

1/2 cup pure maple syrup

In a bowl soak the wood chips in the white wine for 1 hour. Rinse the salmon well. In a blender, combine the olive oil, rosemary, garlic, and 1/4 cup maple syrup, and blend well. Pour the mixture inside and outside the fish. Place the wood chips on a hot grill until they start to smoke. Place a large piece of heavy-duty foil paper on the grill and poke holes in the foil. Place seasoned salmon on the foil paper, and turn down the fire to 200°F (or use a smoker). Smoke for approximately 3 hours or until the fish is medium-rare in the center and well-done on the edges.

grilled corn with chili butter

6 ears of yellow corn in the husk

1 stick of butter

1 tbsp chili powder

1 tbsp garlic powder

salt, to taste

Soak corn in the husks in water overnight. Place the corn on a hot grill for 30 minutes. Peel back the husks and grill the corn until browned. Remove from the grill. In a small bowl, combine the butter, chili powder, garlic powder, and salt. Mix well and serve with the corn.

fire-roasted yams with whipped butter

1 cup hickory chips

1 cup white wine

6 yams

Soak the hickory chips in white wine for 1 hour. Bake the yams at 350°F for 35 minutes or until they are tender in the center. Place the soaked wood chips on a hot grill, and wait for the chips to begin to smoke. Place the yams on the grill for 10 minutes.

fresh tomato salad with olives and orange

6 Roma tomatoes

15 pitted kalamata olives

2 cups fresh orange segments

1 hothouse cucumber, cut into small pieces

salt, to taste

fresh pepper, to taste

½ cup olive oil

SERVES 6.

Combine all the ingredients and toss well.

slow-grilled pineapple
with key lime crème fraîche

1 whole pineapple, cored and cut in wedges

2 cups crème fraîche

¼ cup key lime juice

¼ cup maple syrup

Wrap the pineapple wedges in heavy-duty foil paper, and place them on the grill for 1 hour. In a bowl, combine the crème fraîche, lime juice, and maple syrup. Remove the pineapple wedges from the foil paper, and top them with the crème fraîche mixture. Serve immediately.

minty lemonade

2 cups lemon juice

1/2 cup mint, chopped

1/4 cup maple syrup

1 cup sugar

1 qt water, or to taste

lemon wedges

Combine all ingredients except the lemon wedges in a blender and mix well. Serve over ice, and garnish with lemon wedges.

basil white wine sangria

1 bottle white wine

5 basil leaves, chopped

1 lemon, sliced

1 orange, sliced

1 red apple, cored and cut into cubes

1 pear, sliced

lemon slices

1/2 cup Rose's lime juice

Combine all the ingredients, stir well, chill, and serve.

RECAP

IT WAS A beautiful day and a truly fun gathering. As I suspected, the candy buffet stole the show. Adults and kids alike had fun scooping out candies, guessing how many pieces were in the caramel bowl, and laughing hysterically over the names we chose to place on some of the crystal holders.

The environment really did wonders for setting the tone. Everyone was relaxed, and they stayed much longer than I would have thought. As far as the beach blanket went, everyone wanted a turn playing in the sand. We probably could have done the whole get-together on the long, low table, as I wrote about earlier in the chapter, but I think everyone liked the thought of sitting on the beach and eating some great food, but in reality they were just as happy to go back to their comfortable seats. However, the kids all gravitated to the beach blanket immediately. Next time I will probably set out a few blankets, including one for children only, and really have fun decorating the kids' blanket.

SUMMER PARTY TIPS

1. Freeze your choice of beverage well before the picnic to keep the beverages chilled for the picnic and to keep the food cold. Freeze fruit drinks or even alcoholic drinks with an ice-cream stick in the center, and they become a tasty dessert.

2. Bring storage bags for dirty plates and utensils.

3. Bring one knife to use for your cutting needs in order to cut down on the number of things to bring. Be sure to wrap the knife well in a durable cloth, bubble wrap, or multiple layers of tinfoil so it won't hurt anyone. If you are cutting raw meats, then separate knives are essential.

4. One of my friends turned me on to this idea, which I love: Take one of your small muffin tins and load the sections with sauces, salad dressings, mustards, mayo, ketchup, and the like. In this way, you don't have to bring seven or eight different bottles.

5. Make sure you keep food that can spoil easily refrigerated and shaded whenever possible.

6. Your local grocer should have ready-to-eat food; many carry single-serving portions in their own containers.

continued

7. Pack cold soups with fruit or vegetables in an insulated thermos. They will make great appetizers or cool drinks.

8. Bring lime, mint, or lemon slices with you to put in water to keep it refreshing.

9. Wash your hands before handling food, or use an alcohol-based hand sanitizer.

10. Keep raw foods separate from ready-to-eat foods.

11. Make sure to keep cutting boards and knives that come in contact with the raw meats separate from everything else to avoid cross-contamination.

SUMMER PARTY CHECKLIST

DON'T FORGET THE ESSENTIALS! Before you step out the door, here's a checklist of the items you'll need to execute this outdoor event.

- ❑ Eating Utensils
- ❑ Serving Pieces
- ❑ Sharp Knife
- ❑ Napkins
- ❑ Paper Towels
- ❑ Bottle Opener
- ❑ Corkscrew
- ❑ Cutting Board
- ❑ Spices Such as Salt, Pepper, Ketchup, etc.
- ❑ Blanket (Nylon or Fleece-Lined, Water-Tolerant)
- ❑ Insect Repellent
- ❑ Sunscreen
- ❑ Plastic Storage Bags
- ❑ Trash Bags
- ❑ Moist Towelettes
- ❑ Ice or Frozen Peas or Frozen Soda
- ❑ Camera
- ❑ Portable Radio with Batteries
- ❑ First-Aid Kit

ACKNOWLEDGMENTS

ALWAYS FIRST AND foremost I would like to thank my coauthor, creative director, brand manager, and great friend, Steve Miller. Your faith and drive blow me away. There is no way I could have done this without you. We did it again, my friend! Congratulations. To his partner, Steve Navarro for his unconditional support and for letting us invade his home so often during shoots and meetings. You're the best!

To my family: my father, Eduardo; mother, Mirna; brother, Ernesto; sister, Monica; my niece and nephew, Rodrigo and Monet; and my brother and sister-in-law, Chito and Lisa. Thanks for keeping me calm and centered and helping me to remember where I come from and who I really am. To my god-daughter, Lucia, and all of the Sanders family and extended family. Thank you for bestowing on me the gift of being a godfather! To Cecilia and the Sandoval family for bringing my family and me so much more than words can say.

To my extended family, the Catalina Marquez *familia*. You are my true teachers. You taught me how to celebrate! *Tias, primas, primos, tios, y todos los demas. Los quiero mucho!*

To everyone at *Extreme Makeover: Home Edition*, especially my executive producer, Denise Cramsey; great friend, Herb Ankrom; team leader, Ty Pennington; and all of the design team, who put up with my constantly being on the computer in the trailer, especially my compadre Ed and my wonderful friends Tanya and Paige . . . and, NO, I was NOT watching *Fat Actress!* To the *EM: HE* crews of "boiz night out," especially Steve Crowley . . . thanks for making me have fun on the road! Let's keep dancing! You all know who you are! To everyone else at *EM: HE* for your support and love.

To all of the many fans who send me messages from all over the world. YOU are the reason I can write this book at all! Keep sending me your messages and comments. I promise I will do my best to personally return every one!

To my dear friends that I have not already mentioned: Richard "Cari" Morales, Mark and Ann Roberts and family, J. L. Pomeroy, Richard Perez-Feria, Fabian Plata, Michael Crepezzi, Jesse Acevedo and Demetrius, Alon Shalom, Carrie Merrick, Jerry Bloom, Steve-O, Kevin Finke, Tom Forman, Neil Giuliano, Melissa Givens, Paul Howard, Reyn Hubbard, Carmen Lopez, Ana Olivo, Shalim and Lesley, Greg Pace, Gavin Rember, Matt Vafiadis, Gabriel Reyes, Mike Ruiz, Gaby Tamayo, Adam Ruth, my friends at the Chambers Hotel, Don Winston!

A special thank-you to Michael Anthony Clements for being by my side during this past year. We've come a long way, baby!

To all of the contributors to this book, especially the event planners, Tom Bercu and Jennifer McGarigle, Max Tucci, and a very special thanks to Marley Majcher. Marley, your very special help and your support have added such magic to this book. You ARE a goddess!! To Keisha Beane and Ronnda Hamilton, thank you for helping the book look so beautiful. To the amazing photographers, Kathryn and Bill.

To everyone at Penguin Group, especially to Raymond Garcia. *Muchisimas gracias* for believing in me like you do. You have been an inspiration!

To my XOL team: Jason Carrier, Giancarlo SanMiguel, Desiree Neill, and Sallie Crawford. Thank you for being so supportive and optimistic!!

I want to send my sincere gratitude to Josh Young, the producer of the accompanying CD and to all of the people who added the musical magic that will be the sound track to this book. You have all, once again, made my dream of making music come true! To Paige Hemmis for your friendship and support. Your energy has been an important part of this project for me. I hope that you know that! Love you!

To all of my business team: my attorney and one of my very best friends, David Colden—thank you for always being there for me! I truly appreciate it. To my attorney Rob Goldman. Thank you for your time and effort! To Eric Weissler for your thoughtful contribution. It was a very generous surprise! To my agent, Carlos Carreras, and everyone else at UTA! To Andy Cohan, Jennifer Flynn, and Giancarlo Chersich at my licensing company, ACI. Let's keep it going!! To everyone at ABC/Disney, especially Vicky Dummer and Greg Bell. You are very special! To everyone at Endemol USA for believing in me. To my PR firm, PMK/HBH, especially Britt Reece and Annie Jeeves. Annie, remember to enjoy all of your senses even when you are on your crackberry! LOL! *Gracias!* To Angel Sepulveda, you are an angel! To everyone at AOL Latino, especially Miguel Ferrer and Megan Barreto, for giving me the opportunity to have a voice online! To Chad Serrano for helping us build an awesome Web site! Jackie and Lisa for keeping me organized! Troy Sattler for showing me how to grow! To everyone at Waterford Wedgwood USA and WC Designs, especially Peter Cameron, Lester Gribetz, Regan Iglesia, Marie Valentino, Harriette Martins, Kathleen Moore, and Patrick McCullagh. To everyone at Taylor Paper and the Occasions Group, with a special thank-you to Jean Anderson and Margaret Nelson.

I want to be sure that anyone and everyone that I may have neglected to mention knows how grateful I am for having this opportunity. Forgive me if I've not mentioned you here, and know that I appreciate all of your support.

From my office in Beverly Hills on this beautiful sunny day . . . a sincere thank you from me, Steve Miller, and my whole team!

DESIGN

eduardo XOL

www.eduardoxol.com

8671 Wilshire Blvd. Suite 400,

Beverly Hills, CA 90211

EVENT PLANNERS

Marley Majcher

SPA PARTY

SUMMER PARTY

THE PARTY GODDESS!

Marley Majcher

www.thepartygoddess.com

VENDORS USED:

Town and Country Event Rentals

Owner: Richard LoGuercio

www.townandcountryeventrentals.com

Carmody & Co

Owner: Terry Clougherty

www.carmodynco.com

Jacob Maarse Florists

Owner: Hank Maarse

www.jacobmaarse.com

Waterford Wedgwood USA

www.waterford.com

www.wedgwood.com

www.wwusa.com

Tom Bercu

THE WHITE PARTY
MARGARITA PARTY

Tom Bercu Presents
www.tombercupresents.com

Jennifer McGarigle

Floral Designer

THE WHITE PARTY
MARGARITA FAMILY
Floral Art
www.floralartla.com

Oscar Maximillian Tucci

THE CLASSIC DINNER PARTY
Delmonico, LLC.
www.maxtucci.com

VENDORS USED:
Waterford Wedgwood USA
www.waterford.com
www.wedgwood.com
Designs by David—Florist
Floral arrangement during napkin
preparation

ADDITIONAL CREATIVE TALENT

EXECUTIVE CHEF / Recipe Development
and Menu Preparation
RONNDA HAMILTON

Chomp! Gourmet
www.ronndahamilton.com

PHOTOGRAPHERS
BILL AND KATHRYN WATSON
Watson Photo

www.watsonphotoonline.com

MENU AND INVITATION DESIGNER
KEISHA BEANE

Interiors and Visual Stylist
Kbeane designs
www.kbeanedesigns.com

CD AND MUSICAL DIRECTOR
JOSH YOUNG
www.thedenrecorders.com

| LYRICS BY: | Guy B |
| COPYRIGHT: | www.guyb.biz |

SONG:	"Crazy"
ARTIST:	Renee Myara
WRITER:	Renee Myara
MUSIC BY:	Renee Myara
LYRICS BY:	Renee Myara
PRODUCERS:	Armand Tambouris and Renee Myara

SONG:	"Time Is Flying By"
ARTIST:	Eduardo Xol and Rocio Mendoza
WRITER:	Eduardo Xol
MUSIC BY:	Eduardo Xol
LYRICS BY:	Eduardo Xol and Rocio Mendoza
PRODUCER:	Eduardo Xol
COPYRIGHT:	2000 Eduardo Xol

THE SUMMER PARTY

SONG:	"OK Alright"
ARTIST:	Helios Jive
WRITERS:	Paul Newman, Rich Alick, and Fernanda Karolys
PRODUCERS:	Paul Newman, Rich Alick, and Fernanda Karolys
COPYRIGHT:	2006 Paul Newman, Rich Alick, and Fernanda Karolys

SONG:	"Everybody Stand Up" (XoLeo Mix)
ARTIST:	Eduardo Xol
WRITERS:	Eduardo Xol, Leo Frappier, and Jeff Grimm
PRODUCERS:	Eduardo Xol and Leo Frappier (www.baysounds.com)
COPYRIGHT:	1999 Eduardo Xol, Leo Frappier, and Jeff Grimm

THE MARGARITA PARTY

SONG:	*"Agujita"*
ARTIST:	Katira
WRITER:	Evan Brau and Katira Alvarez

SONG:	*"A Donde Va?"*
ARTIST:	Daniel Jimenez Afanador
COMPOSER:	Daniel Jimenez Afanador
COPYRIGHT:	2007 Daniel Jimenez Afanador

SONG:	"Vamonos" (Remix of *"Ya Llego"*)
ARTIST:	La Verdad featuring Starr Kessell
WRITERS:	Starr Kessell AKA Starr, Robert Melendez AKA Plan B, David Hernandez AKA Unxpected, and Diego Acosta AKA S.I.R.E.
PRODUCER:	Cory Yothers AKA C-Note
COPYRIGHT:	2005 under title *Ya Llego*

SONG:	"Clouds in the Sky"
ARTIST:	Eduardo Xol, Monica Cajayon and Ernesto Torres
MUSIC AND LYRICS BY:	Eduardo Xol
PRODUCER:	Eduardo Xol
ASSOCIATE PRODUCERS:	Ebiut Cervantes and Josh Young
GUITAR:	Willie Lozano
BASS:	Tim Jaquette
BACKGROUND VOCALS:	Monica Cajayon
PERCUSSION:	Ernesto Torres
ENGINEER:	Ebiut Cervantes
MIXED BY:	Ebiut Cervantes

Recorded at The Den Recorders
(Pasadena, California)

www.thedenrecorders.com

Copyright: 2007 Eduardo Xol

Compilation produced for Eduardo Xol by Joshua Young

Mastered by Darian Cowgill